The Tragedy
of Hope and Change

The Tragedy
of Hope and Change

A Handbook for the American Electorate

Christopher J. Warren

To order additional copies of this book, contact:
Xlibris Corporation
1-888-795-4274
www.Xlibris.com
Orders@Xlibris.com
92030

CONTENTS

The Paddle

I am a kayak guide living in Florida. I never in a million years figured I would write a political commentary, but extraordinary circumstances require extraordinary actions. And although I realize the differences between our political parties and have learned to accept their differing ideologies, the election of 2008 caught my attention.

First was the primary: Barack Obama getting overwhelming support from the DNC over Hillary Clinton? A junior senator from Illinois whose past experience was as a community organizer? The second: where did all these union lobbies come from? SEIU, ACORN, Center for American Progress, etc.—who are these people? Third: the Black Panthers were stationed by polling places during this election. I grew up in the sixties and remember the riots and all the news coverage of this group. This is not the sixties, it's 2008. We have moved way beyond those riots of the sixties. The Black Panthers outside polling places in 2008—really? If I were still reading my Spiderman comic books, I would have to say that my "spider-sense" would be tingling, and it was.

Why must we make simple things like voting a racially charged issue? Why should unions and special interests complicate our electoral system so deeply? So often, they just have to meddle in things and make them complex for the perceived betterment of the greater good; or so we think. Take, for instance, the tax code. What a convoluted mess that thing is. Why on earth would we ever think to devise such an abomination of legal gobbledygook? I think the Treasury Department could take a lesson from us kayakers. *Simplify*! What does this have to do with the paddle? Perhaps the greatest lessons come from the simplest places.

Kayaking is a very simple sport. It consists of simple equipment, simple concepts, and an innate feel of your surroundings. Nothing about this sport requires convoluted concepts or perceptions. The funny thing about simple pleasures is that we often overlook them for something more complex because we feel it is more satisfying or somehow better for us. I can't tell you how many times I've been paddling along, and someone in a huge boat laughs at me and says something about how glad they are to have a motor because this looks too much like work. Later, when I paddle past them as they are stuck on a sandbar after the tide has turned or they're out of gas, I just smile and say, "Storm's coming," and watch them woefully look to the sky.

Over one thousand years ago, the Inuit Eskimos devised a method of propulsion for their kayaks. It was called a paddle. It was about three inches wide and about seven feet long and could be carved out of a tree limb, and it kind of resembled a two by four. When the Europeans got wind of this, they fiddled with it for hundreds of years and created a more complex paddle that they claimed would work better. It had wider blades for greater propulsion and a curved face for efficiency, and was able to be "feathered" to help with wind resistance. It became the paddle for the masses, and while all of Europe and the Americas were using this new design, the Inuits continued to use their old standby.

I can tell you from experience the original Inuit design is just plain better. I carved my own Greenland paddle from a cedar two by four, using nothing but hand tools. It is easier to paddle and equally as efficient; and on a long tour, I can keep up with any euro paddle on the market, even the high-tech paddles. I took a group out on a paddle, and one gentleman jokingly called my paddle a "toothpick." By the end of our tour, he said to his friend, "I'm paddling as fast as I can and can't keep up to the guy with that damn toothpick." Needless to say, I just smiled.

The years of effort to change a perfectly good tool proved futile in design but lucrative in marketing. Because the majority of us failed to question the change, we were convinced by the smooth orations of marketers to spend large amounts of our hard-earned money toward this new product. Sometimes we need to realize that just because something is old doesn't mean it is obsolete or ineffective.

Take, for instance, the Constitution. This document holds the simple rules for our society. Even after 233 years, these truths are indeed self-evident; so why are we allowing our government to ignore it? This book will explore these questions through my own personal views and hopefully explain *The Tragedy of Hope and Change.*

FIRST THEY CAME

In Germany, they came first for the Communists, and I didn't speak up because I wasn't a Communist. Then they came for the trade unionists, and I didn't speak up because I wasn't a trade unionist. Then they came for the Jews, and I didn't speak up because I wasn't a Jew; and then they came for me . . . by that time there was no one left to speak up.

—Pastor Martin Niemoller

I t is funny how often history mirrors itself. The sentiments expressed in this poem by Pastor Niemoller speak toward the dangers of an apathetic nation during Hitler's rise to power. The premise is as poignant today as it was in 1946. Perhaps we could reword the poem and make it a little more up to date, if you will indulge me.

"In America, they first acquired the banks, and I wasn't a banker, so I didn't speak up. Then they acquired the automotive industry, and I wasn't an auto worker, so I didn't speak up. Then they came for health care, and I wasn't a health care worker, so I didn't speak up. Then . . . they came for my freedoms . . . and I was not allowed to speak up."

Absolute power corrupts absolutely!

Martin Niemöller - "Persönlicher Gefangener Adolf Hitlers"
Martin Niemöller - 'Adolf Hitler's Personal Prisoner'

Martin Niemöller war Mitbegründer des Pfarrernotbundes und gehörte zu den aktivsten Köpfen der Bekennenden Kirche. Als "persönlicher Gefangener Adolf Hitlers" musste er acht Jahre seines Lebens in nationalsozialistischen Konzentrationslagern verbringen. In Sachsenhausen war er von März 1938 bis Juli 1941 inhaftiert. Die jahrelange Einzelhaft im "Zellenbau" war sehr bedrückend und führte ihn in eine tiefe geistig-seelische Krise. Ab Juli 1941 war er bis zu seiner Befreiung im Mai 1945 Häftling in Dachau.

Nach 1945 prägten die Erfahrungen seines Leidens in Konzentrationslagern wie auch die Erfahrung der Lagergemeinschaft mit Häftlingen anderer Herkunft, Konfession und Weltanschauung seinen weiteren Lebensweg. Er engagierte sich als Mittler zwischen den Kirchen und Völkern sowie in der Entspannungs- und Abrüstungspolitik.

Martin Niemöller was co-founder of the 'Pastors' Emergency League' and one of the most active leaders of the Confessional Church. As 'Adolf Hitler's personal prisoner' he was forced to spend eight years of his life in National Socialist concentration camps. From March 1938 to July 1941 he was imprisoned in Sachsenhausen. Niemöller's years of solitary confinement in the 'prison block' were extremely oppressive and caused him to sink into a spiritual crisis. From July 1941 until his liberation in May 1945 he was a prisoner in Dachau Concentration Camp.

He emerged in 1945 indelibly marked by his suffering in the concentration camps and his experiences of solidarity with prisoners of other nationalities, confessions and political convictions. He devoted himself to acting as an intermediary between Churches and peoples as well as to Cold War détente and disarmament.

Martin Niemöller, 1947

CHAPTER ONE

WHATEVER HAPPENED TO INDIVIDUAL RESPONSIBILITY?

A story, which is very poignant these days, was once relayed to me about our founding fathers. It tells of a time in which the founding fathers were crafting the Constitution in Philadelphia during the summer of 1787.

After a long day of deliberations, it is said Benjamin Franklin walked down the steps of Independence Hall and was approached by a woman who asked, "So have you given us a republic or a monarchy?"

He looked at her and said quietly, "A republic, Madam. If you so choose to keep it." The rest, of course, is history. From that moment on, our early forefathers chose to individually unite together toward the idea of keeping and defending the freedoms for which this republic stands.

For decades this country became the envy of most every other country in the world. Millions of people flocked to Ellis Island to stake a claim to the freedoms this country offered. We became strong—a superpower we were called. We took responsibility for our actions as a country and many times took responsibility for other countries as well. The historians and veterans alike will relay stories of WWI, WWII, Hiroshima, Nagasaki, and the Cuban missile crisis as good examples. Vietnam taught us a valuable lesson. Sometimes others don't see the world as we do, and when our leaders make a mistake and put our nose where it doesn't belong, we have to take our lumps and support the decision. We should revisit this recent past in assessing our entrance into Afghanistan. Perhaps we were dealt an all-or-nothing hand. If so, we need to accept our responsibility, whatever that may be. This can be rectified easily by the electoral process if we get motivated enough to listen to unbiased interpretations of the circumstances which are unfolding. Let us ignore the ranting of a "Hanoi Jane," and look objectively at the task our brave soldiers are engaged in. Then we can effect a positive change through the electoral process.

I remember growing up in the sixties. The Beatles, Mary Tyler Moore, the Rolling Stones, Dick Van Dyke, the assassination of President Kennedy, *Get Smart*, the Apollo moon landing, Martin Luther King Jr., etc. I also remember the shroud of indignity thrown over Washington as Richard Nixon resigned in the 1970s. The greatest lesson learned from him was that even as the most powerful man in the world, you still have to answer to someone and take responsibility for your actions when you screw up. Richard Nixon had to answer to us for his actions. Thank God for our Constitution.

Don't get me wrong, I believe that Richard Nixon loved this country, but he got caught up in the nastiness of politics. I believe his actions were for the betterment of our country, albeit a path guided by political vector. Our future leaders need to understand the simple natural rule of law the Constitution depicts. We need to expressly tell our leaders the *public* dictates what this country should stand for, and we as an electorate need to take *responsibility* for the continued success of this ideal.

LEARN BY CONSEQUENCE

When I was nine or ten, I had a BB gun. The only thing I was able to shoot was old cans. You see, in my household, my stepdad was a hunter. The first rule about guns that I learned was never ever point it at anything you do not want to shoot. The second rule: if you killed anything with it, that item was your supper. If I dared break rule number one, I got spanked, and the gun was taken away. If I dared break rule number two, well, let's just say—steak for them, squirrel for me. These were called consequences.

The funny thing about consequences is there used to be so many of them as rules to be broken. (Today, not so much.) One day I was out in the yard and noticed there were a few broken windows in the barn. I figured, seeing there were already some broken windows and I was sick of shooting cans, no one would care if I shot out a few more with my BB gun. I was sadly mistaken.

When Dad got home, he was livid. He brought me into the house and hollered at me and took the gun away, telling me his dad would have swatted him with a switch. I apparently had a strange look on my face because he asked if I knew what a switch was, and I said I did not.

He then stood up and said to me, "C'mon." We took a walk into the woods, and my dad found a nice green switch and showed it to me. He then brought me to a birch tree and started to whack that tree so hard the bark was flying everywhere. He suddenly wheeled around to me, placing that switch inches from my nose, and growled, "How do you think that will feel across your hind end?"

I was shell-shocked. I mumbled something like "Not too good." And my dad threw the switch away, turned around, and said, "C'mon, let's go."

My eyes were wide, and my heart was nearly tachycardic. We hopped into the car, and he brought me to the hardware store where we purchased enough materials to repair the windows I broke, plus all the other ones. We then went out to the shop for the evening, and Dad taught me how to glaze a window the old-fashioned way. For the next two weeks, every evening after homework, my free time was spent repairing the windows in the barn. Even after forty years, I'll gladly put my skills to the test against anyone. I got threatened with a spanking more times than I could count and was actually spanked maybe twice in my life. The key here is that I knew all too well that follow-through was imminent if I pushed the envelope one smidgen too far.

I tell you this story because *consequences are the road to enlightenment.* We may not understand such logic at the time, but trust me, I know from experience. Consequences require reflection, and reflection breeds understanding, and understanding breeds knowledge. Unfortunately, it appears this country has lost a portion of its sensibility and its acquisition of knowledge, or even worse, just plain common sense. We don't seem to embrace the concept of consequences anymore. We have been lulled into a mind-set that is formulated upon an ideal that states that someone else will deal with the consequences.

Even as a country, we seem to support only mild initiatives, for the name of peace or something else. We do not take a *meaningful* stand against obvious oppressors anymore, and therefore we relinquish our jurisdictions to others and then cry out that we have been wronged. (Perhaps we should remember the actions of JFK.) Yet if we continue with such inaction, we have abandoned our children, ourselves, our neighbors, and our national lifeblood, the Constitution of the United States of America. *Without this, we fail as a country.*

Although my education included a strong dose of American history to include the Constitution, I am ashamed to admit, at the time of my penning this chapter, I did not own a copy of the Constitution of the United States of America. That changed immediately. The next words that I penned, I had a copy of the Constitution, and the Declaration of Independence at my side. This only took a minute—OK, thirty minutes.

"In Congress, July 4, 1776 . . . We the people . . . hold these truths to be self-evident . . . all men are created equal . . . endowed by their Creator . . . are granted certain inalienable rights . . ."

These words fill each and every American with pride and joy, but somehow we have forgotten the advice of Mr. Franklin (if you choose to keep it.) When we are granted any given rights, there must be some responsibility put upon the individual to uphold those rights. If we give up that responsibility, we become a pawn in someone else's game. So if you want to live in someone else's dream, just stay complacent and make sure your responsibility, and your voice, are given to someone else.

Let's take a business model, for example. Hypothetically, I own a small business. I make a modest profit and pay all my bills and taxes. As time goes by, I do not want to continue to invest in the infrastructure that has made my business successful because I am old and tired. I begin to squander my savings on vacations. My business begins to fail. I call my US representative and state that I have been a viable business for the community and deserve a bailout.

In this current administration, my rep says he can help because I'm too important to the community to fail. I do not know where he got that information, and I do not care because I am getting a free ride from the taxpayers. The money comes in, and with renewed energy, I am ready to make investments that will launch my business into the twenty-second century.

But wait! The government has other ideas, which I disagree with; but the government had bought me out with this bailout, and subsequently I am removed from my position. The taxpayers have footed the bill for the survival of a company, which now has no direction nor leadership, and it exists as a shell of its former self, funded by people who don't understand the nature of this business. Hmmm, sounds like GM (yes, this could happen to you).

What went wrong was the fact that I needed to fail on my own. If I chose not to invest in my own company, it's my own fault that I failed. This is my consequence for inaction in the business model. Capitalism allows for companies that do not thrive to fall away by attrition, without the help or financial burdens imposed on the taxpayers. Government has no place in the free market economy. I am sure if my business were to fail on its own, there would be a line of folks waiting for the best deal to invest their money and ideals to achieve their version of the American dream. We need to stay away from micromanaging as a country.

Speaking of micromanaging, I also hail from the health care industry. I can tell you from experience that the move from doctor-based to corporate-run models of the health care industry has done nothing to enhance the cost-effectiveness nor the time-efficiency of the industry. Most doctors will agree.

The real solution is a cap on wrongful death and malpractice, rather than a "cover your ass" modus operandi. Excessive diagnostics simply clutter up the flow of commonsense care and cost billions of dollars each year while being distributed by members who took an oath to perpetuate life with respect, privacy, dignity, and swiftness. Most doctors are willing to take responsibility for their actions based on their expertise, if given modest protections from the Constitution, not edicts from a corporate or government entity that cost consumers and insurance companies excessive amounts of money due to greed and misconceptions about the business of health care.

Again, this is an example of businesses being controlled by those who do not have the experience of the task at hand. Don't get me wrong, the health care industry is in dire need of an overhaul; but overregulation or a national system will lead to absolute power from lobbyists and other special interests, and the only ones who will suffer will be those that need it most. Remember power corrupts, and absolute power corrupts absolutely. Look deeply, my friends, at the current health care "reform" bill that narrowly passed in the first quarter of 2010.

Our founding fathers designed a government based on a system of checks and balances. This system only works when each of us takes responsibility for our actions by keeping our legislators in check. This means making sure they are voting the way we elected them to do, based on the platform they presented to us in their campaign. If they do not, only *we* can take responsibility to correct the situation. If we choose to do nothing, then we reap what we sow, and we will become a Socialist state full of mindless masses denouncing the freedoms granted to us by the Constitution, in lieu of an omnipresent leader with his or her own agenda. We will stand by and watch one of the greatest documents of the world slowly and systematically wither before our eyes. As our freedoms disappear, we will become victims of a corrupt society devoid of responsibility, and we will eventually find our place comfortably in the Third World.

Don't believe me? Watch as our children grow up in a world without consequences, or perhaps veiled threats with no follow-through. Sometimes there may be a thin line between the perception of discipline and abuse; but love, honesty, discipline, and communication are the constant threads our children will respect and understand. Discipline will breed respect, and respect will create character. It was character that led our founding fathers to travel thousands of miles across the Atlantic and fight against an oppressive monarchy to create a new and better land in which to live. Even now the United Kingdom questions our current actions as we slowly move toward a Socialist mind-set. It appears they recognize the benefit of a great republic and wonder why we would ever look to change it, after all the sacrifices began 233 years ago.

So what happened? Why are we beginning to abandon our individual responsibilities and freedoms for a more universal Socialist society? Some will argue it began with FDR's "new order," and they may be right to some extent. After all, the Great Depression called for drastic action, and FDR felt that government had an obligation to the American people. We did subsequently learn that government handouts are only a temporary fix, and real relief comes from a competitive business environment.

But Woodrow Wilson failed to uphold the Constitution and chose a progressive course as well. When WWII began, America could finally move from a welfare mentality to a working mentality, and capitalism was again the road best taken. There was only one small problem. After the war, labor unions began to creep into many trades in the United States. While businesses were trying to compete with each other during this industrial spurt, unions were lobbying for equal and better pay for their workers. Unions grew large and evermore powerful, as did their lobbies.

This action has slowly priced American goods to the top of the markets and has forced the United States to be "creative" in our international trade. To be competitive, we have had to move manufacturing plants overseas to Third World countries or use overseas labor to keep costs down, and this action has upset the unions. Go figure. The unions drove costs for these companies up but do not take the responsibility when the companies have to downsize or move overseas to keep afloat. The vicious circle that has been created is this: labor costs skyrocket, cost of products go up, unions ask for more money to pay their members to buy American, labor costs skyrocket, etc. Until we manufacture overseas and our quality declines, and no one wants to buy our stuff anymore, and we have a trade deficit. No one can afford American goods anymore, and US companies begin to merge or are taken over by foreign entities.

Labor unions have protected the American worker so closely that they operate like little governments over their members. The members pay dues (taxes) to the unions (governments) in return for protection (level playing field) that cripple the capitalist ideal and drive operating costs through the roof. When the businesses try to cut costs or fire unproductive employees, the unions lobby Congress (God) to increase pay and protect workers, all in the name of the American dream. This overpricing and these protectionist tactics force wages and benefits to exceed what the free markets can sustain, and our products become too expensive for trade.

Why do unions lobby a company for a raise? Why don't the individual employees just ask for one based on their merits? Because unions represent a lot of workers, and there is power in the threat of a company-wide strike. It can cripple a highly productive company. The problem with this type of gang mentality is not every worker who is represented is a stellar employee. The unions don't care how you perform as long as you have paid your dues. Bad employees cost companies millions of dollars each year. They should be able to fail on their own and be replaced by more energetic and capable workers instead of being protected by a dictatorial entity and a policy that costs the consumers money. Is any of this sounding vaguely familiar?

The other problem with the gang mentality is that not everyone has to think. There is always someone in the group who will take supervisory charge and maybe promise things that cannot be delivered in the name of keeping the peace, or worse, they may have an entirely different agenda altogether. This lack of individual thought within the group leads to complacency and even laziness. After all, if you never have to ask your boss for a raise based on your performance, why would you work harder than your neighbor? Just let the unions strong-arm the companies and dictate when you go on strike for higher wages, better conditions, etc. The unions must realize that we are *in* a global economy, but we are *not the same as* a global economy. We must price ourselves to nurture our sales but not to succumb to the idea of pricing ourselves out of our market and asking the government to "spread the wealth" toward a Socialist ideal.

I am not really anti-union. I truly believe they have their place in the system, but I question the tremendous power unions have compiled and the ability to feed millions of dollars into the Washington political machine each and every election. Don't get me wrong, the religious right is just as guilty, if not quite as effective; and herein lies the problem: The larger the group, the more single-minded they become and the more easily coerced into one person's ideals.

Individuality begins to wane, and either one of two things occur: the group gets so focused and power-hungry it begins to micromanage everything; or one leader takes charge, and those who would disagree feel too overwhelmed to question the ideal, and they just give up and become complacent because we don't have to be responsible anymore. The unions have adopted a liberal ideal that takes "e pluribus unum" and exploits it exponentially.

They convince workers they are oppressed and need to band together for the betterment of the workforce. Other self-perceived "oppressed" groups have seen this work and adopted the same type of mentality, and the liberal left wing of the Democratic party was the first to open its arms to protect these special interests. No one needs to take responsibility anymore; they just cry foul, and the Washington bureaucrats rush to their aid at the cost of the taxpayer.

The religious right has also begun to learn from this mentality and has created a powerful lobby as well. So have the pharmaceutical industry, the automotive industry, and a myriad of other groups, forming into large masses controlled by only a few and nurturing a "lamb in the fold" mind-set.

Remember the Branch Davidians, that religious cult in Waco Texas? The sweet talk of David Koresh and the isolated lifestyle of the church created an environment where nothing was questioned. This is sort of a carte blanche plate for one man to work his ideals and begin to brainwash his congregation. We cannot ignore the power of Jim Jones and the resulting tragedy in Jonestown of over nine hundred killed by mass suicide in Guyana.

When we rescind our rights to question the validity of our leaders' actions and completely allow them to think and act for us, we open the door for a shepherd, no matter how corrupt, to lead us within his flock. Is this happening to America now? The eloquence of Barack Obama and the controlling force in Congress of the Democratic "yes men (and women)" have led a very complacent country down a road of promises, which will cost the United States its very place in the world through irresponsible spending, deficit mismanagement and possibly some unconstitutional policies. And we have never ever questioned the plan. It is about time for America to wake up! And stop the madness that is being forced so quickly down our throats.

In the early days of September 2009, the principal funding organization for the Obama campaign was ACORN, which has received over fifty-three million dollars in government funding (yes, your tax dollars) and has been under investigation for criminal charges concerning an undercover story raised by two individuals who posed as a pimp and prostitute. They wanted to set up brothels in various cities throughout the country, with underage illegal girls from Central America between the ages of twelve to fifteen.

On September 20, 2009, George Stephanopoulos from ABC's *This Week* asked the president if he had agreed with Congress to cut off all government funding for ACORN. And his response was this: "Frankly, it's something I haven't followed closely. I didn't even know that ACORN was getting a whole lot of federal money." He continued in reference, "It's not the biggest issue facing this country. It's not something I pay a lot of attention to."

How in touch is he with the American people? Fox News had been reporting this story for more than four weeks. How could he not be aware? This is clearly a corrupt organization that is the largest and most influential community-organizing entity in the country. It has shed its veil of goodness and revealed the true skin of coercive manipulation that this shadow administration has to offer.

This is an organization that has been one of the largest contributors to the Obama campaign and an entity that the president even worked for early in his career. How can he be unaware of fifty-three million dollars in government funding and the blatant corruption surrounding ACORN for the previous four weeks or more? Is he just unaware or simply dismissive? How can he make us believe?

OK, enough Obama bashing. Let's get back to *our* responsibilities. I will relay a true story and a poignant example of the progressive mentality of those who could be your next-door neighbors. The kayak shop I worked at is an open-air environment, and in March 2009, a feral cat began frequenting the property. She was skittish and untrusting, and my co-worker, who is a progressive (he'll say Democrat), stated that he was going to buy food for the poor kitty. I suggested that we either leave her alone or call Animal Control for advice. After all, she was wild.

My liberal friend insisted on feeding this cat. After months of constant feeding, the cat started to become somewhat domesticated, and I asked my friend when he was going to take her home. He replied that he could not take her now, but if his elderly dog passed away, he might take her home at that time. In the meantime, my friend got his hours cut, and guess who was now responsible for feeding this cat?

When his dog did pass away, I asked again when he was taking the cat home. And my friend said, "Oh, I can't take her home. She'll just have to be the shop kitty." This means that we all now have to care for this cat when he is not here, because he cannot. Now the business is up for sale, so what happens now? Who will take care of the vet bills? Who will keep this cat healthy? My friend is one of the most compassionate people I know, and I admire him for that, but one cannot just take on a responsibility by oneself and pass that responsibility on to the rest of us (who did not want it), when he decides not to follow through just because his initial action makes him feel good. There are consequences to each action we do as individuals and as a government.

From folks dumping hot coffee in their laps and demanding restitution from the restaurants for their own ineptitudes to bailing out on a helpless cat after insisting that *we* (who—you and the mouse in your pocket?) just have to help her, progressives and leftists pass the responsibility on to the rest of us. Is any of this sounding vaguely familiar? How about those GM folks? Why did we have to use taxpayer money to bail them out? Why were they too big to fail, and how come the person who suggested the bailout doesn't have to pay?

The health care debate is another perfect example. We were told that this will not cost taxpayers a dime, but now Congress is saying the Cadillac insurance plans will be taxed, and Medicare services to the elderly will have to be cut. Why is it that these progressives conjure up these self-proclaimed necessary programs for their special interests but require middle America to take up the responsibility of paying for it, when it will not benefit them and, in most cases, cost them? Indeed, whatever happened to individual responsibility?

CHAPTER TWO

LET'S SAVE THE NEXT GENERATION

I t sounds almost Democratic when you speak it aloud. I think Nancy Pelosi would be pleased. The only problem is, I want to save our youth from the ideals of the Left. Back in the days of the William Jefferson Clinton era, Bill's wife, Hillary, took to the podium one day and proudly uttered the immortal words, "It takes a village to raise a child . . ."

Now, I am a fan of Mrs. Clinton. I believe she is very intelligent, has good intentions for this country, and is doing an adequate job as Secretary of State in this administration. I also believe many other people have uttered words they subsequently regretted. Let's review: "'I am not a crook' . . . 'There are WMDs' . . . 'I did not have sex with that woman' . . ."

I am convinced of the sincerity of Mrs. Clinton's words, although it seems a large portion of villages raising children seem to be situated in Third World countries or cordoned off and led by corrupt ideologues. I am thinking this model is not in the best interest of the United States unless we want to canter down the road toward Third World Socialism.

For those of you who want to stop reading right now, just indulge me for one more statement. Fortunately it does not take a *village* to raise a child, it takes a *parent*. When we give up the responsibility of molding our children on a daily basis, we leave that child to the devices of a portion of society we know very little about. Day in and day out, we leave our children in the hands of caregivers because we are too busy and financially strapped to stay home anymore.

Our society has become so overly litigious, the caregivers cannot discipline our children when needed, and the seeds are planted daily to create the spoiled child syndrome that our parents warned us about. In order to learn limits, children continually test us. Without boundaries based on consequences, children will continue to test and push the envelope beyond what is acceptable behavior. Different methods work for different children. Spanking may work for one child where a time-out may work for another. When we prevent the folks whom we trust to care for our kids the ability to enact our choice of discipline, we teach our future society to disregard consequences and do what they want without fear of punishment or responsibility.

Growing up in our house, we had a three-strike rule. You got warned three times. If you didn't learn, you accepted the consequences. When I was a child and I swore, I was taken to the bathroom, and soap was rubbed across my teeth. It didn't hurt me; it was just plain unpleasant. If I hit anyone, I was spanked just enough to make it sting a little. After the punishment, my parents (usually Mom) always came up and talked about why I was punished and why my behavior was improper. We used to have a word for that—it was called discipline, a combination of corporal punishment, lessons, and love. It was not abuse. As a matter of fact, it hurt far less than falling off the swing my mom told me not to stand up on, or sticking my finger in the live light socket, or touching the hot stove Dad had warned me about.

We have gone way overboard in this protectionist mentality perpetuated by the "it takes a village" folks. I remember one parent told my mom that she did not spank her child because it would hurt his little psyche (thank you, Dr. Spock). The last I knew of him, his mother had lost control, and he ended up in juvenile hall. There are people in our judicial systems who allow lawyers to argue cases of corporal punishment as true child abuse cases. In some situations, a rebellious minor child is allowed to file the case, as some bureaucrat who knows nothing of the circumstances surrounding the case acts as a surrogate (it takes a village.) Many times these kids are taken from their parents, bounced around the system, and sometimes spend a good portion of their time in and out of the penal system at taxpayer costs.

Now before the letters start, let me say there are many parents who cannot handle the responsibility of raising a child and should use some viable form of contraception. There also is a definitive line between corporal punishment and child abuse. It just seems that we have let the smooth talkers of the legal system reach deep into our emotional psyche and make us forget that we can think for ourselves—"It takes a village to raise this child. Let me, a powerful bureaucrat, represent you." Remember sometimes the hard road may cost you emotionally, but the easy road will almost always cost you financially. The future state of this republic stands with the children we are raising at this very moment.

How's that for responsibility? No pressure really, if you want to live in a Socialist country. However, if you choose to keep this republic which was crafted for us 233 years ago, then it's time to get with the program and stand up for the rights and freedoms granted us by our forefathers. It is time to start teaching our children proper societal values and responsibility that will simulate true democracy.

We can start by ensuring our children understand and value consequences. It is important to instill swift punishments if needed, and follow through on our punishments for misbehavior. It is important to teach them never to start a fight, but always be ready to finish it. Our children need strong values and strong positive role models to emulate. We need to show our children honesty, strength, remorse, and most importantly, love. If we implement all these tools effectively, our children can begin the journey to the world our forefathers intended, where peace, strength, and freedom are the tools for success. This of course leads me to the issue of education, or the lack thereof.

It was not too long ago that children began their education in kindergarten, then grades one to twelve, college, grad school, etc. I'm not too sure if I agree with the whole "preschool or prekindergarten" concept. It appears to be nothing more than glorified babysitting to free up more time so parents can get back to work sooner. The less time we as parents spend with our children in their formative years, the more we allow them to accept the values of others without our supervision.

I do believe that kindergarten is the proving ground for social adaptation and is the precursor for the development of proper behaviors in the structured environments of the classroom. Because of the transitional nature of kindergarten to include a social and learning environment, I expect the teacher to be part educator and part babysitter.

When the child reaches first grade, my belief is the teacher should be solely an educator. If the teacher has to spend most of their time with discipline, we as parents have not done our job. It is not the educators' job to consistently have to be disrupted to discipline our children; although we as a society seem to have placed such burdens upon them. If your child is not socially advanced enough to maintain discipline in the class they are assigned, perhaps they need to be sent home or perhaps even held back a grade. We have to understand that each child may develop differently, and some may have barriers like ADHD or other developmental challenges, or perhaps we just did not instill enough discipline in their upbringing. Either way, a child held back a grade is not the end of the world for either the parent or the child. Communication is needed between the parent and educator with a focus on the child's continued development and success. This should not be confrontational in nature but a cohesive agreement on what is needed for this child to succeed on the global stage.

The Department of Education was originally founded in 1953 as the Department of Health, Education and Welfare, and became its own independent cabinet in 1979. You see, bureaucrats in Washington rhetorically claim education as a necessary arguing point to win elections. After all, everyone wants our children to excel on the worldwide stage of academia. In 1953 Dwight D. Eisenhower created the cabinet of HEW to oversee many of the domestic issues affecting everyday Americans.

In 1979 Jimmy Carter, at the request of the Democrats, made the Department of Education its own cabinet post so Washington could better oversee the national progress of education in this country. It appeared the United States wasn't holding its own compared to the rest of the world in education. Making a cabinet to deal solely with the national issue of education made a lot of sense back then. The department could work to set national standards in education so each state had the same goals; they could oversee curriculums to keep pace with the rest of the world and hopefully raise the bar so American children could compete equally on the European and Asian stages.

Alas, as so often is the case when Washington gets involved in issues, cabinet directors get pressure from Congress, which gets money from lobbyists, etc. Add in a healthy dose of special interests, and everything goes to hell in a handbasket. It has recently been reported the Department of Education is now contemplating setting the standard for a passing grade for the GED to 40 percent. According to fairtest.org, the United States is the only economically advanced country to rely so heavily on multiple standardized tests, which give only a limited amount of data. Most other countries use performance-based testing, where they are evaluated on real work to include essays, projects, and activities.

The No Child Left Behind Act came to fruition in 2001 and mandated that each state should set some standards based on guidelines from Washington for standardized testing. Hence the MCAS, FCAT, MCAT, TAKS, etc., aptitude tests were introduced for each state, to monitor how our children were doing as they progressed through school. These aptitude tests have been around since the early decades of the twentieth century, but in 1996, the Reagan administration had asked for a greater concentration on education. The Clinton administration followed suit, as education is always a smart political issue to connect with the electorate. This would have been a great start if there were just some way to assess the information in a productive way.

This law allows for each state to individually set scoring for the testing. It mandates that each state tests certain grade levels in certain subjects such as reading and math, but each state scores the tests differently. If the students achieve a passing grade, their communities can get federal funding for education. Now take this so-called standardized testing within a country that is a self-proclaimed melting pot, add in a dose of the NAACP, ACLU, various affirmative action groups, and any other powerful lobby with a special agenda, and you begin to get the picture of what a mess this can turn into.

Let's take a child who is from another country and has immigrated here legally, but his command of the English language is limited. English is not the official language of the United States, so it is not required for citizenship. Our foreign friend is entered into high school and fails the reading portion of the standardized testing and is required to stay back.

Enter the ACLU. They feel an injustice to the child was done because he has limited skills in English, but his scores were otherwise fine. They lobby the State and cry discrimination. What happens then is truly an abomination. The State crumbles to the pressure, and lo and behold, the standards for the aptitude tests drop lower and lower with each and every case put forth before the States, or even Congress. Because the federal government has made these tests mandatory and awarded subsidies to cities that follow the recommendations, school systems around the country have begun to fail systematically, even though in some cases, statistically a higher percentage of kids have passed. There is a real fear that teachers will begin to cave to the pressure and teach to the test, not the students' needs, so as to achieve a greater passing percentile and maintain the federal dollars for the school system.

In an article by the Associated Press dated December 2010, the headline read, "Nearly 1 in 4 fails military exam." The article goes on to say that nearly 25 percent of qualifying high school students fail the entrance exam (ASVAB) for the military. Quoting a report from the Education Trust, "Too many of our high school students are not graduating ready to begin college, or a career, and many are not eligible to serve in our armed forces." The scary thing is they *are* graduating.

The article goes on to cite an example of a typical question on the Army ASVAB exam. "If 2 plus x equals 4, then what is the value of x?" Almost 25 percent of our graduating high school students get this type of question wrong. And the tests for the other branches are slightly more difficult, according to the article.

We have as a society seemingly embraced this bait and switch tactic that leaves us pacified and our children woefully underprepared for the challenges ahead of them. Certain regions of the country are worse off than others, and perhaps that has to do with the economic demographic of the region. Quick comparisons are rather difficult as each state uses a different formula for calculations, and even with some tenacity and basic math skills, one can hardly compare percentages between states.

Take Florida, for example. They used a mean scale scoring system from 100-500 for each subject and then calculated the percentage of passing students. Massachusetts calculated percentages for these select categories: proficient/advanced, proficient, needs improvement, and fail. Then they calculated a comprehensive proficiency index (passing percentile.) Massachusetts also tested for Reading, Math, and Science, where Florida only had results for Reading and Math. The percentile comparisons of tenth grade Reading were this: Florida had a mean scale score statewide of 305 out of 500, resulting in a passing percentile of 51 percent.

Massachusetts had a passing percentile of 90.3 percent, with 23 percent above proficient. The results for tenth grade Math were eerily similar. Florida had a mean scale score of 327 of 500 and a passing percentile of 57 percent, while Massachusetts had a passing percentile of 86.7 percent, with 43 percent above proficient. (Sources: *http://fcat.fldoe.org* and *http://www.doe.mass.edu/mcas*)

There appears to be such a disparity between the States. Neither State uses the same method of reporting, so we might assume there is no continuity between them in the testing process. It could be that a proficiency rate of 51 percent in Florida could very well be equivalent to the 90.3 percent in Massachusetts depending on which formulas are used. The problem here is each State is competing against each other with different scoring parameters. We must adopt a standard formula nationwide so we can compare our national results with other nations on the world stage.

I did however take a look at the sample questions for the tenth grade reading exam for both States and found the readings and questions to be of similar level, albeit different subject matter. One could ascertain that there is some level of continuity for these exams, although I question how these test materials compare with other nations around the world.

We are in a global environment. It is not enough to set standards that just make us feel good and bolster our preconceived notions of self-esteem. *We need to be able to compete on the global arena!* We need our children to intellectually make us feel inadequate, as we continue to learn until we die. I am not talking about how fast they can text-message or any other secondary skill they can master. I'm talking about cohesive understanding, conceptual vision, and artistic interpretation.

Complacency is not an option. If we are to compete on the world stage, we need to take charge both as parents and as a nation, to ensure our children do not fall into the quagmire of egotism and complacency that has defined America in its recent past. Someday I want to have a comprehensive conversation with a sixteen-year-old who can offer an opinion of hybrid technology, instead of predicting who will be the next "American Idol." This is what every American should wish for when we speak of the next generation.

Unfortunately it doesn't stop at high school. Many colleges and universities house educators who believe and practice theories which may or may not be similar to yours. I am in full agreement in the practice of educating our children in the concepts of other nations and cultures that are different from our own in the name of knowledge. I disagree when ideals and opinions are taught as fact, and our kids are indoctrinated in the beliefs of their professors and mentors. My Catholic child should be educated to the world of Judaism but not necessarily indoctrinated to believe it. The Socialist teachings of Marx and Lenin should be explored for historical reference and comparison to the capitalist ideal, but it should not be deemed a better or worse ideal. That should be left up to the student to ascertain its viability.

It is up to us as parents to make sure these educators are not indoctrinating our children, and make sure our children get an unbiased presentation of these controversial issues throughout their educational career and the freedom to assess them objectively. That comes from talking to your children and becoming aware of their education all the way through college. Simple conversations about their ideals will be enough to realize if they are thinking with a clear and unbiased mind.

I do want to be the alarmist in the room, but we must realize that the biggest influences on our children, besides their parents, are educators, caregivers, clergy, and to some extent, their bosses. These people are held in high regard by our children, and they have a great opportunity to influence our children's belief system. Our children see them as educated, successful, and charismatic. The less time we spend with our children, the more time these folks have to shape an impressionable mind.

The human mind is like a proverbial sponge from birth to about the age of twenty-five. After that the brain continues to develop, but many of our social and religious values have begun to solidify and are less easily manipulated. Childhood and adolescence become the time where values can be most easily affected by outside influences. This is why many believers in the Socialist agenda like Van Jones, Cass Sunstein, and George Soros find jobs in our colleges and universities. These highly esteemed and charismatic educators and clergy members such as Rev. Jeremiah Wright wish to affect the values of our children before those values become hardwired. It is very important to keep abreast of what is being taught to our children in the name of education.

The First Lady whom I admire very much seems to focus a lot of attention on our children while trying to overcome the problem of childhood obesity in this country. I will be the first to say this is an admirable endeavor by the First Lady, and who doesn't want our children to eat healthy? The White House garden is a marvelous tool to educate our kids to the benefits of eating healthy. It is a wonderful thing for the White House to set a good example for the rest of us to emulate, just as long as it is an example, not a mandate.

We should hope that this example is not slid into legislation behind our backs from the Department of Health and Human Services. Why? What would such a program end up costing the communities? You see, broad-reaching legislation affects us in ways we don't imagine. A revision of the school lunch program, for example, might just cost us a bundle. Think for a moment of the difference in cost between a bag of organic carrots and a bag of regular carrots in the store. If the government mandates healthier, more expensive foods for our school lunches, the cost trickles down to the states, then the cities, towns, and finally the school districts.

Guess who finally gets to pick up the tab? What may be considered a cost-effective lunch program for someone making four hundred thousand dollars a year could really financially hurt someone who makes forty thousand dollars a year. Perhaps rather than changing the school lunch program at taxpayer expense, parents could buy healthier choices and let their children bring their own lunch to school.

This of course was an example of how we must examine broad-based legislation when it gets presented to us. This scenario is not being played out in Congress, but easily could be.

When we hear of progressive legislation to help us *all,* think for a moment of how it may actually affect *you.* When a bill gets passed that leaves "no child left behind," is it really going to benefit your child in the end? Do we really want our children to think and act collectively, or independently? Remember, one in four high school graduates cannot pass the ASVAB test for the military. Think about it.

CHAPTER THREE

THE TRAGEDY OF "HOPE AND CHANGE"

E very day I get people from all walks of life who want to explore the wonderful world of kayaking. One of the questions I get asked is, "Am I gonna get wet?" The tragic thing about this is I get asked this question a lot more than I

should. My first response to this was a hearty laugh, which was taken as an insult. My second response of just a quizzical look did not fare much better. (Apparently I was not in line with political correctness.)

My current response is, "They call it a *water* sport for a reason." I tell you this because keeping upright in a kayak on flat water is simple physics and balance. Truly it is equally easy, or easier, than balancing on one leg. Yes, you will get wet, mostly from paddle drips or splashing (after all, you are on the water in a shallow paddle craft), but rarely from capsizing. Most people who capsize do it either getting in or disembarking from their kayak.

The reason they capsize is quite simple. Usually they put the V-shaped bow or stern on the hard flat surface of the boat ramp and stand up in the boat, making their center of gravity very high upon a very unstable precipice. This is the equivalent of placing a ruler on edge upon a table and trying to stand on it. The success ratio is approximately equal.

I actually have had people show up to kayak in dress pants and dress shoes. One gentleman tried a kayak out on a demo day and proceeded to lean way over in the kayak, and he systematically capsized. When he resurfaced, I asked him what he was doing, and he replied, "I wanted to see how stable it was." He then complained he lost his glasses, and his wallet got soaked.

I just couldn't show any sympathy and said, "Well . . . silly you." This did however render some applause from the gallery. I still see people who put eight-hundred-dollar-cameras around their neck and hop into a kayak in saltwater. Some of them even refuse a dry bag and get so angry when their camera gets ruined. Go figure.

I used to wonder what prompted people to do these things without even the most remote thought of consequences. Then it hit me. *We don't have to think for ourselves anymore!* The lawyers, lobbyists, and Washington bureaucrats will think for us and protect us if they want to keep getting elected.

If I am too stupid to realize that hot coffee should never be placed on my lap while driving and I burn myself, I just call my lawyer and blame it on the restaurant. He gets a bunch of other people who are equally as lazy, to petition the court system, find a judge up for another term, coerce some lobbyist to pad the election coffer, and lo and behold, a huge settlement and new labels on coffee cups.

Somehow we have been lulled into thinking that our ineptitudes are not necessarily our fault, and we do not have to wear the coat of responsibility because it may hurt our interpretation of self-esteem. We talk ourselves into this cocoon of protectionism rather than face embarrassment, and the smell of untold wealth permeates the air until the legal hounds or special interests can formulate a case against those who have worked honestly and hard to make a living, and they are financially dismantled in the name of the greater good.

Let's take the Madoff scandal, for example. Bernie was a crook of unscrupulous measure. But he was very good at what he did. He was able to foresee the end of his plan and subsequently gave away or invested a lot of the stolen money to many unknowing people prior to his being caught. When he was caught, after his son alerted  authorities, there was only a fraction of money left for restitution. So in the name of fairness and equality, the AG, our beloved Eric Holder, and the federal government went on a witch hunt to recoup the money the not-so-savvy investors lost. It seems anyone who knew Madoff, or even those who shook hands with him, were harassed, investigated, and monies collected for restitution.

On December 11, 2010, Bernie's son Mark committed suicide by hanging himself in his apartment in Soho while his two-year-old son slept in the next room. Why? Because Eric Holder and the US government continually and relentlessly harassed him and the rest of the family with frivolous lawsuits aimed to recoup money those who invested with Bernie had lost. The Associated Press even stated in their newswire that neither of Bernie's sons knew anything of the Ponzi scheme and have never been charged with a crime.

The Madoff business was two-pronged. Bernie worked the investment side, which was described as being under lock and key (the Ponzi scheme,) and the two sons worked the legitimate securities side from a totally separate office. The attorney general's investigation proved that there was no connection between the two sides of the business and admitted the sons appeared to have no knowledge of what their father was doing. Even so, the AG continued to harass this family and their friends solely because they had money. This could be categorized as "redistribution of wealth"—our government using its power to forcibly take money from the wealthy and give it to those duped by their own unwillingness to become smart investors. Bernie Madoff was a predator and deserved everything that he got, but we can't forget his "victims" voluntarily invested with Madoff, perhaps without the proper amount of research necessary. Now sadly, the office of the US attorney general has blood on its hands.

Bernie Madoff was able to get away with this for so long because there was so much deregulation instilled by the right-wing politicos in Washington. We all want businesses to thrive, but when the fox is watching the proverbial henhouse, we now see what went wrong with the banking industry, the auto industry, and the financial sector—CEOs spending huge wealth for their own vacation homes, investments in foreign banks, and huge bonuses even with taxpayer-bailout money. In other times, we would call that skimming, continually taking off the top while investors reap diminished returns, workers get miniscule raises, and consumer costs continue to skyrocket.

On the other hand, the left-wing politicos feel too much corruption lives within the capitalist system and have come around to strictly regulate almost everything they can get their hands on, and supposedly give the money to more deserving folks (like campaign contributors.) They have created a czar for this and a czar for that, claiming that certain businesses are too important to fail and need a taxpayer bailout. The question I am not hearing from the masses is, how do we pay for this? And what will it do for our economy? It appears both parties are engaged in a game of overcorrection. We have too much of this policy and then too much of that.

The tax debate of 2010 is a good example of how the Democrats perceive the mistakes of the Bush deregulation policy and want to "help the middle class," to overcompensate for their own greedy spending policies.

Following the Socialist ideal of redistribution of wealth, the Obama administration wants to raise taxes on families making over $250,000 a year. He claims that it would lessen the burden on the middle class and make the millionaires or, as he calls them, the "uber-rich," pay their fair share. It is a known fact that those wealthy Americans are responsible for creating economic growth and jobs for the rest of us. The Obama administration seems to think the wealthy are somehow different than us, perhaps not quite human or perhaps they think totally different.

You see, to understand this tax issue, we must apply the concepts to our day-to-day life. If we the middle class have our taxes raised from 20 percent to 35 percent, what is the first thing we would do to make ends meet? One of the first things we do is tighten our belts and stop unnecessary spending. This of course puts less money into the local economy because we buy less locally, and this stifles economic growth. The small pittance of money I contribute to the economy is negligible of course, but the wealthy contribute much more because they can.

Amazingly they think just like you and I. When their taxes go up, they also tighten their belts and stop unnecessary spending and look for more economical investments, usually overseas. The wealthy shop around for the best deal, just like you and I do. It just has more of an impact on the economy than my paltry expenditures. You see, the wealthy don't live on another planet as the left-wing politicos and mainstream media darlings want you to believe. They are your neighbors who own businesses, create jobs, and invest in local economies if the government will let them operate. Why then would you want to raise taxes on the wealthy?

Lower taxes for everyone can help to stimulate the economy. How do you pay for that? Begin with a reduction of government and wasteful spending, and utilize a budget to live by. I suggest a flat tax. Believe it or not, 15 percent of one million dollars is more than 15 percent of fifty thousand dollars, so the wealthy will actually pay their fair share. Isn't simple mathematics amazing? The government needs to take a lesson from the wealthy and the middle class—get a budget, pay your debts, and stop trying to create class warfare to promote socialism.

THE KAYAK TEST

When I take people for kayak lessons, one of the first things I do is to put them in a kayak, give them a paddle, and then observe them as they paddle to the classroom area. I have given them a briefing about paddling, but that is all. The reason I do this is because I can learn a lot about how much a person listens, understands, and utilizes innate processes to finish the trek. Many times people just zig and zag back and forth from one side of the river to the other crying for help. They overcorrect with each stroke, never learning to soften up the stroke so they don't keep bouncing from side to side. They never learn to "feel the waters."

Kayaking is mostly about feel and the observation of one's actions. With just a little observation and experimentation, the average-thinking human can usually begin to see how action equals response. For the people who have difficulty grasping that concept, I don't place blame on the individual. I blame the slow influx of protectionist values (don't let them fail or get hurt!) and bias of the mainstream media.

For so long now, we have been at the mercy of special interests trying to keep the playing field even and slowly dismantling our educational system to make sure "no child is left behind." This has bred a society who would rather cry foul and wait for a rescue than think for themselves. We no longer have to question, so therefore we do not think outside of the box. Many times I believe we don't think at all. Unless we are told what to do and when, the why is unimportant.

For those people who continue to zig and zag across the river, my advice is to stop whining, take the responsibility to listen to your instructor, and trust your consciousness because learning will then come easily.

The tragic downfall of America is a combination of many things: first and foremost, the feel-good attitude behind the "no child left behind" policies of the Department of Education; second, the polarized views of both political parties, which results in the overcorrection of policies already in place.

Our founding fathers created policies for the people, even though they may have had personal differences. Our representatives in both houses of Congress have seemingly lost sight of the country as a whole, in lieu of their own party's agenda. Special interests and a bias of the mainstream media have taught us if we cry hard enough about a perceived injustice, someone will take up our cause, and we won't have to take responsibility. And with a never-ending supply of money finding its way into Congress, corruption and bias are rampant.

Third, I am finding that personal and political bias has begun to infiltrate our classrooms. Again, many populist ideals are tossed around without question or fair discussion toward their validity on many campuses across the country.

When I was in college, one of my professors had each member of the class read an article, write a commentary, and then discuss our findings. My assigned article was about the atrocities of radiation experiments conducted on humans and animals in the fifties. The article was very biased toward the damages done to people and the fact that our government would let this sort of thing happen without recourse.

I was the only one in my group who challenged the conventional slant and wisdom of the article and touted the experiments as necessary to establish current radiation reduction policy in the United States. I claimed that the benefit far outweighed the cost, and these people who were tested were not even viable members of society at the time, as they were death row inmates or terminally ill animals.

The discussion got very heated that day, and the instructor said not a word. She simply turned my paper over, gave me an A, and quietly went back to her seat to continue watching me defend my case against a rabid and venomous audience. The thing I noticed to this day was the fact that not one of my colleagues dared to side with me that day against the conventional, populist ideal, even though I had presented valid facts and reasoning to question the bias of the article. This is the kind of "mob mentality" that leads to quick but possibly improper action. If such biases exist in our classrooms, do they seep into our justice system as well? Is justice truly blind and unbiased, if our judges are taught populist ideals in college?

In the case of Justice Sonia Sotomayor's ruling on the Connecticut firefighter's case of reverse discrimination, was blind justice really served or were we just setting a new low standard to enable the Socialist ideal of Saul Alinsky to seep into the American psyche? Just because no ethnic firefighters passed the promotion testing, Justice Sotomayor ruled we should not promote those who did pass, in the name of ethnic equality, and suggested the test should be revamped. I have to say, if we lower the standards for promotional testing, would those who passed really be getting a promotion? And can we be sure they can actually handle the added responsibility? Perhaps we will just promote overpaid and underqualified individuals into our most important positions. Maybe we should think about how we will be affected down the road.

Subsequently a Connecticut panel of judges overturned Ms. Sotomayor's ruling, and all who passed the test got their promotion. But be afraid of these progressive thinkers; our complacency can give them the "shoo-in" to affect policy that will change us forever. Remember President Obama wants to "fundamentally change America." Now that Justice Sotomayor has been in the high court for several months, has she indeed adopted a more unbiased view toward society? It is something we need to keep abreast of.

There used to be a phrase used around the campus at college: if you can't dazzle them with brilliance, baffle them with BS (not a bachelor of science degree). This adage works perfectly in American politics. Political issues usually are so convoluted and filled with legality that even the above-average citizen has a difficult time deciphering them. Just watch a congressional hearing on CNN. This doesn't mean that we as US citizens should be kept out of the loop; after all, isn't that what the mainstream media is supposed to do, *report fairly without bias and help us to understand the confusing mumbo-jumbo so we can make informed decisions?* Of course it is.

The main problem is, they do not. We as a society accept the drama and fanfare of celebrity in more aspects of our lives than you might think. Our news have been changing to our demands of more dramatic stories, to the point of repetitive coverage of only the most dramatic, albeit ridiculous, aspects of the day. In other words, we are fed point without the counterpoint. Fair politics does not sell as well as Hollywood drama, and no one knows that better than the American political parties. They have slowly been baiting the media with alarmist politics since Watergate.

We crave dysfunction in our lives. Just look at the programming we continue to watch on TV, such as *Big Brother* or *Survivor.* We actually have a full evening of programming on one station devoted entirely to animated comedies. These shows exemplify the dysfunction in our society. They are filled with crude confrontations between what are supposed to be average citizens spewing multiple expletives in each sentence.

It reminds me of a statement my grandmother once said about my own potty-mouthed antics as a child, "Only uneducated people use those terms because they don't know the proper terms to use and cannot express themselves correctly. They simply don't know any better." As I grow older, I feel my grandmother may have hit that one right on the head. There appears to be a direct correlation between the lower grade of education and the higher amount of expletives spoken in a conversation. Don't get me wrong. I am also guilty of the aforementioned offense, which makes me question further.

The "tragedy of hope and change" is not about stupidity. As members of the blue-collar comedy tour have reiterated, "You can't fix stupid." But lo and behold, you can fix ignorance. Ignorance is bred from complacency, and if we can motivate the electorate to be more proactive in their thinking and prevent Socialist demigods from downgrading our educational system so no child is left behind, we can again be the superpower we once were. The strong shall teach the weak to stand unassisted.

I know this sounds a bit creepy, but unfortunately television and the mainstream media are now the greatest formative means for our society, not education. Whoever manipulates the media can affect the pulse of the country. My dad used a phrase that is so true these days. He would describe complacent, lazy, ignorant people as being "fat, dumb, and happy." Orwellian as it sounds, our country is grossly obese, woefully undereducated, and we sit steadfastly munching pizza watching animated sitcoms for an evening of entertainment. We have become lambs in the fold, not wanting to think for ourselves, under the ideals of a government controlling way too much and moving much too fast.

CHAPTER FOUR

WHEN ELOQUENCE IS KING

How can he make us believe?

Eloquence. It is such a beautiful word; it sort of rolls off the tongue like silk slides off your skin, smooth and easy. Eloquence is even more impressive when delivered in a particular tone, like the deep resonating voice of the late Paul  Harvey, or Mr. J. Peterman, the character in *Seinfeld* played by John O'Hurley. Eloquence can be defined in a word as persuasiveness. It doesn't have to be delivered in a deep baritone like J. Peterman or a boisterous sermonlike tirade the likes of the Rev. Jesse Jackson. Sometimes the soft-spoken folksy approach can win the hearts of millions, as was the case for William Jefferson Clinton.

In the early days of journalism, the story that broke first got the most attention. If you were a newspaper, radio, or TV station good enough to consistently break the latest story, you were on top. As faster communication made competition so much closer, a new criterion was needed to define success. Where seconds used to define success from failure, image became the new measuring stick for the ages. For the kings of radio, the voice was all-important. If it caught your attention and boomed with an air of professionalism, ratings went up.

In television, it was a whole new ball game. The image of the consummate professional was all-important. It also helped if you had that convincing voice as well. I have noticed that the 1980s saw the most significant and rapid change in the presentation of our news. When Ronald Reagan became president, his presence onstage carried over to his press conferences, and he made us feel warm and cozy. He almost had a fatherly demeanor that was firm yet protective at the same time. His successor, George H. W. Bush, and his wife, Barbara, made us feel like the folks next door were in the White House. The image makers would advise the use of some popular phrases like "read my lips, no new taxes!" which had the whole country cheering. This lighthearted approach to connect with the masses slowly began the change in mainstream media. By the time the Clinton campaign had achieved the presidency, Bill Clinton's folksy, "boy next door" approach had America and the press eating out of his hands.

The morning news shows in the 1970s, which were about news first, had now become more about entertainment than news. What used to be a news program with entertainment segments now was an entertainment show with a news segment. We became enamored with the first president who played sax on *Saturday Night Live*. He became more of a rock star than a world leader, and the press was on a whirlwind love affair with this president. His smooth talk would assuage and persuade Americans to believe everything was all right.

The stock market soared, and new jobs were created. They may have been low-paying service sector jobs, but a figure is a figure nonetheless. The White House press secretary and crew were known as "spin doctors," ably and adeptly telling the American public just what they wanted us to hear. We were told the deficit was being reduced and jobs were being created, but we did not hear of the foreign interests slowly and quietly buying up American companies as we outsourced industry and sent our tax dollars toward debt reduction. It is like a person who wants to pay down their mortgage by selling everything they own. They now own their house, but the house is empty, and they are sleeping on the floor.

The Republicans appeared to recognize the paper economy of the Clinton era and embraced a cohesive agreement with the idea that war will bring us together as a country. Find a common enemy, rally the troop support, and begin to create jobs. WWII had certainly helped unify the country after the Great Depression. The problem with this is war costs money. Enter George W. Bush. He narrowly won the presidency from Al Gore due to those dreaded hanging chads and realized he would be a one-term president if he couldn't make his mark in dramatic fashion. Although both candidates had little eloquence and charisma, even the wooden Al Gore had his pet issue, climate change, and successfully began hammering this issue to the public. Yet from a charismatic standpoint, he actually made "W" look good.

President Bush finally found his issue after September 11, 2001—Al-Qaeda. What came next still has me a bit baffled. We went from the focus of Osama Bin-Laden and Al-Qaeda to Saddam Hussein, Iraq, and weapons of mass destruction. It appears that if you can't charm the masses with eloquence, just scare the bejesus out of them with bad intelligence.

President George W. Bush was about as awkward and uncomfortable as one could get in front of the camera, next to Richard Nixon. President Nixon loathed the media and tried his best to stay away until that fateful interview with David Frost. President Bush did not have that luxury. Over the last fifty years, the Republicans have had few candidates able to compete with the Democratic media darlings the likes of John F. Kennedy, William Jefferson Clinton, and now Barack Hussein Obama.

Oh sure, the Republicans had Ronald Reagan and—well, Ronald Reagan. It remains a fairly accurate statement to say the GOP is still wallowing in the past when it comes to media expression. Even during the infancy of the Kennedy administration and before the demise of "Camelot," someone in the DNC realized that the public infatuation with this handsome charismatic president and his wife was something which was going to last. The Democratic Party has studied the impression the media makes on public opinion to great effect. They understood how iconic characters are created by a hungry and competitive media who strive for the advantage that keeps them on top, and they cater heavily to them.

As the once razor-sharp edge between journalism and entertainment continues to dull in the mainstream media, both parties have grasped the concept that the public would rather watch fourteen days of funeral arrangements for Michael Jackson or reruns of *Big Brother* than listen to a two-hour debate on federal policy that could greatly impact their lives. When the antics of Paris Hilton and Lindsay Lohan's return to rehab make the first story on the news, or worse, a half-hour segment on *ET*, we the public are in an intellectual vacuum, or severe denial. It is shameful of the media to cater to that tragedy of society, but the DNC more than the RNC realize that our society is enraptured with idols.

Let's face it, politics is boring, and I would like to think both parties know it. The Democrats just seem to understand what to do to market their ideas to the public. Simply create the impression of an iconic candidate, and let the icon-loving media cover it twenty-four hours a day. Eloquence and charm work much more effectively than the straight-talk express. Broad sound bites filled with ambiguity, delivered with confidence, and a good story of success or compassion, seem to get the job done.

The Republicans are slow on the uptake and present themselves as the Order of the Neanderthals. Oh sure, they exploited "Joe the Plumber" albeit too late, and they embraced Sarah Palin as the poster child for the new Republicans; but she was ill-prepared to take on the Clintonesque Democrats. She was willing and able, but when she started to falter, the GOP abandoned her by the proverbial side of the Alaska Highway. A bad move for the GOP, as Sarah Palin is a quick study. She had injected energy and a charisma in a failing party but lacked a concise message to overshadow the Democratic media machine.

It did not help that she was paired with a member of the old guard in John McCain. At seventy-two, his image was too much of a dichotomy against either Sarah Palin or Barack Obama. Had the 2008 presidential ticket been more like Mitt Romney and Sarah Palin, I believe the election would have been much closer or very different. Let's face it, the Democrats took a junior senator who was a community organizer in his recent past career and sold him to the public as a viable presidential candidate. On paper, he didn't stand a chance against Sen. John McCain. Obama was a Harvard graduate and a community organizer with no business or executive experience on his resume; and McCain was a senior senator, war hero, and had far more life experience. So how did Obama win the presidency? Image is a powerful thing when you have an electorate as complacent and uneducated as ours. Substance takes a backseat to eloquence.

The Bush administration had beaten a dead horse with the Iraq war and the much lamented "war on terror." Americans wanted change all right, but I never expected them to elect a president based on change that was never explained. As the Republicans asked questions, Obama used the broad brush of ambiguity to spread the message of hope and change, and the media never asked the pertinent question, "Explain what you mean by change?" Apparently they were taken by Mr. Obama's smooth deliberate orations and his sleek appearance as he flowed across the stage.

Sen. McCain unfortunately seemed out of his element in a formal debate, sometimes flustered by the questions and seemingly trying to gather his thoughts, as he lumbered around the stage, a hero whose war injuries had taken their toll. It is my belief that most of America failed to listen to his words but were too engrossed in the image disparity between the two candidates.

Then Sen. Obama had huge amounts of money coming in to his campaign, mostly from large organizations like the ACLU (American Civil Liberties Union), NAACP (National Association for the Advancement of Colored People), and ACORN (Association of Community Organizations for Reform Now). All these organizations have been tied to helping people in our society perceived as disadvantaged, and all are in strong support of the Democratic Party. These groups went out at the request of the DNC and targeted first-time voters with broad promises of change and hope. They convinced them they were "disadvantaged" under the Republican ideal, and the "candidate" for change would lead them out of the darkness. There was even a woman on the news in Florida, who stated that under the Obama administration, her mortgage finally would be paid off. I'm sure she got a rude awakening after the first six months. I'm not saying they lied to her, but if the message was so ambiguous that she got that idea, we need some drastic change in our educational system.

The American people have elected two presidents into office, neither of which has had a detailed plan to support their campaign pledges. President G. W. Bush got us into the longest two-pronged war in American history without an exit plan, and President Obama pledged to solve our economy without revealing that it will cost the taxpayer much more than the $787 billion stimulus package and the absorption of many banks, Chrysler, and GM, to date. Both these presidents cost the American taxpayer huge sums of money either in elevated taxes or huge deficits, which devalue our dollar and lead to inflation.

When we accept a plan without asking the obvious questions, we are at the mercy of either eloquence reigning supreme or our blatant complacency or both. As we become more complacent and less willing to question the motives and ideals of our potential leaders, eloquence and ambiguity become the most effective means for implementing special agendas. If they can feed us a broad plan of hope and change, keeping the masses fat, dumb, and happy, our individual freedoms can slowly be replaced with a Socialist plan that will level the playing field for the "greater good."

I find the dismantling of individual freedoms not "good" at all but a step toward a meeker America, a country that has acted in accordance with a world order not of its own volition but to the assumption that independence is evil or haughty; and we are asked to assimilate into a kinder, gentler, global union that leaves us vulnerable and unprotected. Call me silly, but didn't our founding fathers sail across the Atlantic to escape a single-minded oppressive government controlled by a monarch engaged in special interests for the perceived "greater good?" Isn't that why they crafted the Constitution, to ensure we never ever fall prey to another institution like that? Perhaps each and every one of us should give it a second look, and maybe ensure that our children get a healthy dose of American history in elementary school and again in high school.

We need to remember that freedoms granted to us by the Constitution and the Bill of Rights are ours *only* if we should choose to keep it. We must not fall victim to the flowery and eloquent orations declaring "hope" and "change" in subliminal exchange for our inalienable rights. We must listen closely to the press conferences played before us.

One of the easiest tests I have found to determine if we are being baffled by BS is to ask simple questions and wait for a concise and simple answer. There are two ways to avoid answering a question. First, answer only in one-word answers. Second, answer in long, convoluted, broad answers that leave the questioner with more questions than answers. Unfortunately the average person cannot be at these press conferences to ask the simple questions, and we unfortunately have to rely on the members of the press who rarely ask clear, concise questions.

One of my liberal friends asked me what I was doing as he watched me at the keyboard one day, and I answered I was writing this book. He then asked what it was about, and I replied it was a political commentary. At that moment, he started on a tirade stating that what all the wild conservatives want is to round up the evil liberals and destroy them, and the Republicans were going to ruin this country. He then stated, "Barack Obama has done more for this country in the first six months than GW Bush had in eight years."

I found that to be a rather loaded statement, so I queried, "Exactly what has he done in the first six months?"

There was a lot of stammering and stuttering, and finally he blurted out, "He . . . he's working on health care!"

Actually, President Obama had done a few things in the first six months, just not anything considered outwardly positive. He had bailed out the banking industry at taxpayer expense and overtaken GM and Chrysler. Just think, the government actually owns OnStar. He also took a trip overseas and came home with no treaties signed but had apologized numerous times for various things he seemed to feel the United States was accountable for. All these presented with the same eloquence he used to win the election. I just hope the other nations were as equally impressed as our electorate. As far as I can determine, the president did make mention about health care, but I do not believe at that time he had actually started working on it.

The overseas trip really speaks toward how we as Americans can be swayed in such large numbers by the perception of hope and change. As I read reports in various newspapers and television stations, I did not get the idea that these other countries were swooning in the streets over the speeches that were given by the president. It seems to me in these countries that action speaks louder than words. Take the latest elections in Iran, for example. President Ahmadinejad is a fairly well-spoken gentleman, but when he stated he won the election, Iranian citizens took to rioting in the streets. Now I am not suggesting anything like that for the US electorate, but why do we blindly accept the statements of President Obama without question? It is because we are impressed with his delivery.

Take "Gates-gate," for example. The president took the side of his friend Professor Gates without all the facts and stated the Cambridge police acted "stupidly" in the arrest of Professor Gates. Afterward he then went on TV to say he should have "calibrated his words differently." The mainstream media accepted this as an apology, when in fact it was not. Calibrate means to attune or adjust finely. In this case, it does not change the stated thought, it just fine-tunes it. A calibrated statement may look something like this: "The Cambridge police acted unintelligently."

Eloquence is used to mystify the public into thinking things are different than they truly are, and this administration is a master at the art of eloquence. It is something we the electorate must be acutely aware of, so we do not fall victim to the wiles of corruption. John McCain had it right; we need legislators who will communicate from the "Straight Talk Express."

CHAPTER FIVE

THE BILL OF RIGHTS

T he Bill of Rights of the United States of America is the first ten amendments to the Constitution of the United States, placed before Congress in 1789, ratified by a two-thirds majority in 1791, and authored by James Madison. It clearly states the people's rights under the Constitution of the United States. These first ten articles define to this day the  rules of law as it pertains to each and every American. *These rights belong only to those who are native-born or naturalized citizens of the United States, and only on sovereign US soil.* It is no wonder every year there are tens of thousands of immigrants taking our oath of citizenship every Fourth of July.

Each of us need to re-familiarize ourselves with these articles and realize how precious these rights are to each and every one of us. They are more than just words they are what separates America apart from any other place in the world.

Amendment I.	Freedom of speech, freedom of the press, freedom of religion and right to assembly, right to petition
Amendment II.	Sovereign state, right to bear arms
Amendment III.	Protection from quartering troops
Amendment IV.	Protection from unlawful search and seizure
Amendment V.	Right to due process, double jeopardy, self-incrimination, eminent domain
Amendment VI.	Right to trial by jury and rights of the accused, speedy trial, public trial, and right to counsel
Amendment VII.	Civil trial by jury
Amendment VIII.	Prohibition of excessive bail, and cruel and unusual punishment
Amendment IX.	Protection of rights not specifically enumerated in the Bill of Rights
Amendment X.	Powers of States and people

No offense to any other country, but these ten articles to our Constitution are what keep us from being a country like North Korea, China, Venezuela, or Iran. These sovereign rights are ours to protect; and if we do not pay attention, they can and will be slowly dismantled behind a smoke screen of deception provided by others who have a different idea of what America should look like, perhaps behind the broad brushstroke of "change."

Let us take, for example, the second amendment: the right to bear arms. You may not like firearms, but the amendment does not say you have to keep them, but we as a country are *allowed* to keep them if we so choose. There are laws in place that govern the use of such firearms so the public is protected, but if we are threatened by another country, we have a right as citizens to protect our sovereign lands.

Some people in America and Washington feel that firearms are dangerous and should be regulated, rationed, and perhaps even outlawed. The Obama administration and its supporters are trying to pass a concealed weapons bill that will outlaw concealed weapons from crossing state lines. Mayor Bloomberg of New York City had a press conference to weigh in on this subject, touting his support for the bill, stating that it would prevent criminals from carrying weapons across state lines and therefore protect the public. There is a very true statement that reads, "If we outlaw guns, only outlaws will have guns." The reason people get a permit to carry a concealed weapon is for personal protection in places like, say, New York City. These permits are granted to us under the second amendment.

Many truckers who make a living on the interstates of this great land need this right to protect themselves while on the road doing America's business. This legislation will cripple commerce as we know it today by leaving these truckers vulnerable to crime on our highways. Mayor Bloomberg and those who seek to climb on the populist bandwagon fail to see both sides of the issue and commence to sway the electorate into believing that we can give up our constitutional rights without the dire consequences that do indeed exist.

Let's try Article VI, the right to trial by jury and rights of the accused; before this went into effect, anyone could have you imprisoned for accusations circumstantial in nature. If I didn't like my neighbor, I could accuse him of, say, theft; and he would be hauled off to jail, no questions asked. Without that right in effect, anarchy would wreak terror all over the country.

Most of these rights are to protect us from an overzealous and corrupt government wanting to control all aspects of our lives. Luckily for us, the Constitution has a clause in it that protects the citizens from absolute power. Most changes to the Constitution require a two-thirds majority to pass the House of Representatives, and the laws in this country must coincide with the Constitution as well. Each new law or policy that is put before the House has to be voted on, and then has to go to the Senate for a vote before winding up on the president's desk for approval. This in its simplicity is called a system of checks and balances. It makes it difficult for one party to have complete control of legislation or the Constitution.

Unfortunately the system is flawed. If there is more than a two-thirds majority rule in the Congress and the same party controls the White House, all bets of checks and balances are virtually off. The safety switch here is a *proactive* electorate. You see, we have to be able to change and amend the Constitution as our society changes; because otherwise, we would be following some very antiquated rules. It should not be easy to amend this document unless there is overwhelming support from the electorate, so we need to look closely at this past election.

We the people elect who we want to represent us in the Congress. We cannot be forced to vote for a particular candidate, but if we do not pay attention, we can be coerced by special interest groups to vote for the candidate they recommend. Just look at the effect ACORN had in the "get out the vote" effort for the Democratic Party this past election. This political posturing by special interests and lobbies can allow for all three sections of the legislative branch to maintain a majority (presidency, Senate, and House). When that happens, it is possible for that party to push through almost any legislation they wish. It also puts the Constitution at grave risk. This is what Ben Franklin meant of our republic when he said, "If you so choose to keep it." It is a fact that a government by the people and for the people needs the people to remain aware so as to thwart covert attempts to undermine the basic rights of the citizenry.

Some states, for example, have the individual right to set up road blocks for DUI checkpoints. If I am forced to stop at this checkpoint whether I am intoxicated or not, would that action be considered a violation of the fourth amendment? Could it be considered coercion and unlawful search and seizure? No one argues that DUI is a crime and a public safety issue, but it is reminiscent of the pre-WWII days in Germany: "Your papers, please." This action is disguised as protection for the public, but it reeks of Fascism as the government weeds out its chosen subjects. Is this unconstitutional? Or is it protection for the public good?

Florida allows the police to fine people who are not wearing their seat belts, although they had to stop that individual for another violation first. Now under a new law, the police have the right to stop and fine you for not wearing a seat belt as a separate violation, just by observing you as you drive by. This came about because a few people petitioned the state concerning a passenger who was thrown from her car after an accident and died due to the ejection. Is this just mere protectionism or Fascism worming its way into our freedoms? After all, a seat belt is really a personal choice for adults except in the case of our responsibility to the children in our care; or is it?

These issues need our scrutiny. Those few folks thought they were doing us a favor, but at what cost, and is the change really going to amount to anything but an increase in the coffers of the state? It may seem like a minute issue, but remember big changes start with baby steps. Sometimes our individual rights, whether they appear good or bad, just must be upheld for the true betterment of our country and the protection of the Constitution.

Many States have tossed around the idea of sin taxes lately. States use various reasons to heft higher taxes on controversial products we as citizens use every day. Florida just levied a one dollar tax on tobacco, basically to meet budget expectations. Other States have considered it based on the edict that it will help to prevent our children from smoking or help prevent lung cancer. These are all good reasons to quit smoking, but I do not want the government to get involved in our personal habits even if those habits might kill us eventually.

Similar tax hikes are being considered for alcohol (did we learn nothing from Prohibition?), soda ('cause our children are too fat! Thank you, Michelle Obama), and some special groups would like to tax birth control pills and contraception to promote an abstinence-only edict for our teenage children, which by the way has been studied and proven not to prevent teenage pregnancy at all. Abortion is still a hot-button issue in this country, and many will argue the pros and cons, but the *right* to choose is still constitutional as explained by the *Roe v. Wade* ruling by the Supreme Court. (Do you see how corruption begins to worm its way into our laws?)

Our individual freedoms are always going to be challenged by those who do not agree, but we must stay vigilant. My personal habits and beliefs do not have to mirror yours, but my right to practice them without infringement should be upheld equally as much as your right to disagree.

In the recent past, we have had a fair balance between the executive and legislative branches of government, which has allowed a rather slow progress of passing legislation but a fair debate of issues and the implementation of just policies based on the general support of the public. In 2008, the public became enchanted with the cries for a different direction and the change promised by the Democratic opposition. The Republicans were systematically replaced with Democrats in both houses of Congress, and by November, we had elected a Democratic president who was the proverbial son of the union-controlled left wing and friends to some self-proclaimed Socialists. Now we have a situation where the presidency and both houses have over a two-thirds majority, and with virtually no ability to filibuster, the Republicans are near powerless. The very fabric of our country lies in the hands of Barack Obama, Nancy Pelosi, Harry Reid, and the huge special interest money machine which has gotten them elected. Watch your freedoms very carefully. Luckily the electorate got motivated by the Tea Party movement in the 2010 election, and the House went over to a Republican majority, but continued vigilance is necessary to keep a balance of power.

Legislators have an obligation and desire to please their respective political parties, especially during elections. After all, their views are essentially the same. Unfortunately this republic is not homogenous; and therefore the views of either party may not gain full support of all of the citizens of this great nation. The two parties each represent an ideal for America, albeit different. When an elected official wins his or her race, from that point on, they are obligated to the *people*, not the party. The party's job is done, for the most part.

The cloak of partisan politics must be shed in the sacred name of the union. They must no longer cater to the campaign and special interests but to the desires of the American people. The "boys of summer" who got you elected today don't matter tomorrow. The betterment of the American people is your duty now. Listen to them, and focus on how our Constitution can shape America to be the model for the world. This is the American interpretation for our legislators, presented by our founding fathers and adopted September 7, 1787.

A poem by John Lygate once stated, "You can please some of the people all of the time and all of the people some of the time, but you can't please all the people all the time." We know politics is messy. I certainly do not expect every piece of legislation to get my full approval. I do however expect my rights under the Constitution to be upheld unequivocally by both parties. If I do not agree with some policy which has passed, I can contact my representative and ask them to argue on my behalf. That is what makes America great. I do not want the Constitution at risk by those who would be at the beck and call of the special interests, which brings me to the subject of czars.

At last count, the Obama administration had thirty-two czars and counting. The term "czar" is derived from the title "tsar" to designate Russian, Bulgarian, and Serbian monarchs of pre-WWI Europe. In the United States, the term "czar" is an informal title for a certain high-level executive branch official who oversee or direct federal policy on a given topic or who coordinate policies between different departments on a given topic (wikipedia.com).

The problem with a "czar" is they can affect policy without the cumbersome consent of Congress. They are appointed by the president and do not have to be vetted by the legislature and therefore do not have to answer to the legislative branch. So who's in charge of checks and balances? It appears to me that if an administration desires movement on a number of issues, it should stand up and bring these desires before Congress, instead of appointing special advisors (czars) behind the legislators' back. It is my concern that anyone appointed to a high government post without the consent of the republic (i.e., the legislature) seems suspect or covert at best.

Are these appointments actually constitutional? Do they indeed benefit this republic? These questions need to be answered. The answer to the first question is yes, they are constitutional. Some of these czars hold cabinet positions, but many of them do not, yet they are high-level advisors to the president and do not require vetting by anyone. President George Washington had four Cabinet posts in his administration, and G. W. Bush had fifteen. The first czar, I believe, was appointed in the seventies as an "energy czar" to combat the oil crisis of that era. We need to ensure that these people are vetted by the FBI and confirmed by Congress, who is supposed to represent you. If they are not, we need to speak out *loudly*!

Many of the czars in the Obama administration have very questionable histories, and they have the ear of this president. Their influence can direct the president to veto legislations that do not meet with the ideals of these czars or to modify legislation which will directly influence us, without representation from our appointed representatives. Big government is a complex and dangerous entity, which allows corruption to grow, with no safeguards for the general populace.

We must read and understand these ten rights and pay close attention to what bills our legislature is passing, to make sure they pass what I call, the Bill of Rights litmus test. If they do not, then it is up to us, and only us, to throw the bums out, take back *our* country legally, peacefully, legislatively, and again begin to make America the icon of freedom, peace, and democracy for the world.

CHAPTER SIX

TO REGULATE OR NOT TO REGULATE, THAT IS THE QUESTION

When a person comes into the shop and wants to go kayaking, they have a choice. They can go on a guided tour or a self-guided tour. You can think of a guided tour as a regulated tour. You are regulated by the guide as to where you will paddle and how fast, and if you don't know how to paddle, the guide will take you under his wing. It gives you a feeling of security, but you are somewhat controlled by the guide. A self-guided tour could be considered an unregulated tour. You can go where you want and as fast as you please. If you don't know how to paddle, you are learning on the fly.

Some shops regulate you very tightly on their guided tours. They make you paddle in single file and listen to the guide's oration. Some shops regulate you only enough to ensure your safety and comfort, and let you interact with the guide along the way. I have seen some other shops that leave customers on their own right after they sign the release for self-guided tours. Our shop regulates you to wear the safety equipment and gives you advice on where to go based on your experience, for our self-guided tours.

The difference is liability. We live in a very litigious society, and for some businesses to survive, we have to cover our proverbial hind end. I am a true believer in absolute freedom, but if I left some people who come to kayak to their own devices, there could really be a catastrophe. So how much regulation is too much?

The Republicans will tell you that deregulation will and does stimulate the free market economy. The Democrats will tell you that only tougher regulations can keep control of abuse. Both parties are right, but neither one will back off from their lobbying constituency to come to a viable agreement, so back and forth we go from administration to administration, regulating, then deregulating.

Look what happened during the Bush administration when the Republicans deregulated the banking industry. Power-hungry CEOs skimmed off the top, gave themselves huge bonuses, and virtually bankrupted the system; and Capitol Hill turned a deaf ear. We cannot allow Washington to let the special interests run amok to accumulate obscene profits while their companies are operating in the red. We also cannot allow the government to absorb industries and bail them out with taxpayer money, or worse, print money to pay for it. This just devalues the dollar and increases inflation. So what should we do? Let's take a lesson from history.

Many years ago, a lot of engines that were manufactured had a device on them which was called a governor. It was placed on engines that did not have any indicators to inform the operator if it was running outside of the preferred parameters. Its purpose was to regulate the RPMs of the engine just enough so it would not overheat or overspeed. Many times it was set at the factory and set considerably lower than the max level the engine could safely run. It allowed the operator of the engine to run it without having to think whether he was going too fast or not. Basically, it was idiotproof.

When I was in the service, I drove a twenty-seven-ton fuel truck. We were given trucks with governors on them so our speed was kept at a specific maximum of five mph, for safety reasons. I found this to be interesting due to the inherent risk of attack. If we were on the flight line and a Pearl Harbor-type of attack occurred, five mph will allow us to be a slow-moving bomb just ripe for the picking. Wouldn't it make sense to remove the governor so we could escape the area more quickly if needed? The government was more concerned with controlling speeding issues on the flight line than the potential damage a bunch of five-thousand-gallon "jet fuel bombs" creeping among the aircraft could possibly cause. If they removed the governors, there would no doubt be those drivers who would break the rules and cause chaos.

Oversight, not regulation, would be the logical solution. Patrol the line, fine or remove the offenders, and keep the regulation to a minimum. In the case of businesses, the stockholders should be the folks who oversee the operations of a business.

I relay this story because the word "government" has the root "govern" in it. To govern is to *regulate*. Using the above metaphor, we can clearly see that the more the government gets involved in free market economics and the more taxes are levied, the more bogged down businesses become and the less competitive they are. Now if we take a business like AIG or Fannie Mae, run by a CEO who is constantly running above their maximum limit, we can have a crisis similar to what we experienced in the housing and banking crash. How do we end up preventing another business from falling by the side of the mismanagement highway? We could govern it and not allow it to reach its potential, or we let them fail. If the failure is due to internal corruption, I say let the chips fall where they may.

Now when a large company with a considerable market share of investors is on the brink of collapse, the current administration feels it is too big to fail and uses taxpayer money to give them a bailout, increasing debt and raising inflation. In the case of the banking bailout, there was no oversight, and the government does not even know where the money went. It probably is not wise to have these large corporations fail, yet instead of just watching and doing nothing, perhaps government could require companies to lay down some indicators to keep investors in the public sector aware of when the company is approaching the proverbial "red line." Let the investing public determine what the company should do next, by giving them some warning before the crisis hits. Perhaps they could require bonuses in publicly traded companies to be put to a vote by the investing public.

A smart investor can tell when a company's management is getting too fat. Make this practice of transparency for investors a requirement for the business to receive a tax incentive, government contract, or tax breaks. This makes it comfortable for a business to run at a fast, profitable speed, yet safely just below the thin red line of chaos. It also makes the investors responsible for how much incentives are given to the upper management. This form of steering moves companies toward a new direction, which is less about regulations and more about incentives and allowing the market to determine success or failure.

Incentives are used to guide companies toward a broad pathway where they have room to breathe rather than follow a tight line with little wiggle room, all the while giving the investor some form of protection or choice in case the company decides to go under. It also allows the corporation the chance to remain solvent in the United States, instead of being forced by our government to merge with a foreign entity, as in the case of Chrysler Corporation.

Regulation forces a company to follow a whole new set of guidelines for the day-to-day operation of the company. Business as usual does not exist. In the case of GM, President Obama had replaced the CEO and dictated to the company the type of automobile they will now begin to produce. I may be out of line here, but what does a community organizer really know about the US market share of automobiles, and is a bureaucrat really qualified to run one of the largest car manufacturers in the world?

This is the fundamental fault with full-blown regulation. Regulation is employed when an entity feels there is an incapability or ill desire to function on one's own agenda, and therefore regulation is "an authoritative rule or order issued by an executive authority of a government having the *force of law*" (*Merriam-Webster Dictionary*). This is what monarchs, Fascists, Communists, and Socialists use to maintain order and power. This is the weapon of a czar—the total control necessary to topple the free market system. It is the ideal our military uses to train and maintain our troops so they can function efficiently under strict discipline. It is a *tool* necessary to train our troops, not a way of life, at least not the way toward free enterprise. This is what our founding fathers declared our independence from and fought for: our right to *life, liberty, and the pursuit of happiness.* If we continue to support a government which practices complete regulation as a means of controlling companies, we will no doubt be headed down the slippery slope toward socialism.

Obviously we need some control, such as overseeing large corporations that do business with the government, so as to reduce the blatant abuse seen from the Bush administration. But we do not have to squelch the day-to-day operations of said companies with government regulations, which cater only to the desires of the Socialist ideals dictated by either wing of the Democratic or Republican Parties.

The health care proposal by the president is a great example of the Socialist ideas of this administration vacuuming up our individual choices. The president suggested that we all can have a choice of accepting universal health care or keeping our current options. Good. I like that. Then he went on to state that when you decide to change doctors for whatever reason, you must then select the government plan as your next choice. No choice of another individual plan is offered. What this does is slowly push out private health care selection in favor of government-run health care.

I have lived overseas for a couple of years, and let me tell you our current system is far better even with all its faults. Just talk to our neighbors across the northern border, and you can see they try to come here for their health care. No one from the United States makes the trek to Canada for their health care. Some will argue that "socialized" medicine (let's call a donkey a donkey) is better than what we see in, say, Mexico; but a freshman med student with a scalpel is better than what you can get in Mexico or any other Third World country.

What we need is reform, and reform is not regulated universal health care. Reform comes from identifying problems in the systems and applying changes without a complete restructuring of said policy. Remember oversight is not total regulation. Oversight would entail something like realizing the costs of health care are directly attached to the skyrocketing costs of insurance companies pushing for litigation and the pharmaceutical companies pushing for newer drugs at twice the cost.

The government could suggest caps for wrongful deaths and a competitive market policy for drug companies to bid for contracts to keep the market share from spiraling out of control and ignoring the lobbyists who control them. Perhaps we could extend to the insurance companies the same right to extend services between States and increase the competitive market share. That would be oversight, not regulation, or socialism. Sure, it would mean less money in the campaign coffers for Democratic and Republican candidates but perhaps lead to a kinder and freer country in which to live. We cannot continue to live with a noose around our neck and expect that everything will turn out like "Mayberry RFD."

Mayberry RFD takes work. As cheeky as it is, it still is the personification of the American dream. The oak-lined streets, friendly neighbors, and peaceful settings continue to tug at our heartstrings even if we live in the urban ghetto. If we are to achieve what every country in the world strives for, we must set the example by limiting the amount of regulation to only what is necessary to curb abuse within the free market system, without total government control. Socialistic practices will only achieve a level less than what we expect from the American dream.

We have been experimenting with various modes of control and regulation for some time now, and if we are to understand where this is going, we must begin to realize that this is indeed happening. I have just read a report from the AP newswire from Rebecca Boone concerning DUI campaigns in Idaho and Texas. The headline reads, "DUI campaign uses forced blood tests." According to the article, this is a federal program to determine if blood draws by cops can be an effective tool against drunk drivers in the aid of their prosecution. It seems the refusal rate for breathalyzer tests have led to more drunk driving trials in the State, and the prosecutor feels this action will curb the amount of trials in the state. If the National Highway Traffic and Safety Administration have their way, this practice could be implemented nationwide. So what is the problem here? Apparently it is illegal to hold a suspect down and force them to take a breathalyzer, but according to the Idaho State Supreme Court and the US Supreme Court, officers can forcefully take someone's blood. Are your eyes bleeding yet?

The nation's highest court ruled in 1966 that police could have blood tests forcibly done on a DUI suspect without a warrant as long as the suspect showed reasonable suspicion of intoxication, and it was done after an arrest and carried out in a medically approved manner. This use of the ruling is egregious on so many levels. First, if the US Supreme Court ruled that this behavior could take place in a medically approved manner, why do the police have to be trained to do this? Why wouldn't they take the suspect to a medical facility unless they are going to draw blood in the field? If they intend to forcibly draw blood in the field, doesn't that violate some sort of sterile environment/safety ordinances somewhere? Is the hood of a police cruiser considered a medically approved location? (Think of all the dead bugs, bird defecations, and spit from the last victim!) Never mind the violation of the fourth amendment—illegal search and seizure. (Yes, I disagree with the US Supreme Court.)

To make matters worse, the officers are trained under a variation of the same program the state's clinical phlebotomists use but under a highly compressed schedule, and some of the curriculum is cut. (Oh, goody!) Nicole Watson, the College of Western Idaho phlebotomy instructor teaching the officers, stated they are trained to draw from the crease of the elbow, the forearm, and the back of the hand. If none are available, then they will take the suspect to the hospital. Ms. Watson continues that they are making quick progress. The training will be completed when they complete seventy-five successful blood draws.

Once they are back on patrol, they will perform draws on any suspected drunk driver who refuses a breathalyzer. They will use force if needed, such as getting help from another officer to pin the suspect down for the draw. Read your history books, my friends; this is *Fascism* straight up.

If one were to study *The Communist Manifesto* written by Karl Marx, one would get an idea of what a utopian society would look like. Unfortunately we have observed through history the unavailability of such a utopian ideal. Humans are flawed. Therefore we cannot adhere to the strict criteria necessary to achieve pure ideological Communism, because it is far too restricting. The closest level we can achieve is to settle for Socialism, which will leave us in a complacent void similar to what we have observed in Europe.

Throughout the sixties and seventies, we have succumbed to the pressures of a select few who have gained in their own movement toward a more equal society. Mostly for the good of our society, and I think a step for the better. We have learned much from the teachings of Dr. Martin Luther King Jr., Malcolm X, Billie Jean King, Rosa Parks, and others who have pleaded their cases and enlightened us to their plights. Our open acceptance of these individuals has also opened the door for a more covert type of individual to gain a foothold and who begins to organize for a more manufactured or perceived group of oppressed citizens. They were not only the racially oppressed, the religiously oppressed, the gender challenged, but now the economically and politically challenged.

By the early 1970s, Saul Alinsky had written an entertaining classic on grassroots organizing called *Rules for Radicals* (1971). Alinsky began with this statement, "What follows is for those who want to change the world from what it is to what they believe it should be. *The Prince* was written by Machiavelli for the haves on how to hold power. *Rules for Radicals* is written for the have-nots on how to take it away."

According to Saul Alinsky's *Rules for Radicals*, in rule number five, "ridicule is man's most powerful weapon. It's hard to counterattack ridicule, and it infuriates the opposition, which then reacts to your advantage." This Marxist ideal states that one should identify the enemy, isolate them, and ridicule them until they are seen as "non-thinking" individuals. This is what is happening within the electorate these days. The DNC has denounced the reaction to the town meetings that have sprung up during the legislative break as an "angry mob." This is evident in the debate over the health care bill. By calling the GOP (and other) supporters of these patriots as "non-thinking people" and an "angry mob," they are following the Marxist rule.

No one wants to be labeled, and it promotes more anger and irrational behavior from those who are attacked. (Just think of how you would feel if I called you a liar.) This public outcry falls in line with the media-supported interpretation of inferiority, and it paralyzes those who oppose the current administration. Perhaps the DNC is systematically trying to stir the pot of anger among the electorate to the point of overheating and allow the president to come and "rescue" the electorate with a crush of the "iron fist" or a version of "Martial Law," filled with his own version of what is best for America. This may seem conspiratorial in nature, but I feel conspiracy theories are indeed possibilities.

Capitalism with all of its flaws is still the best avenue to achieve the true American dream. Let us embrace certain regulations to prevent abuse; but let the free markets nurture, control, and prevail. Only then will we nurture our economy and begin the slow steadfast trek toward again being the superpower we once were, working with other countries to promote freedom and free enterprise. Mayberry RFD may be considered a utopian snapshot of the past, but it was a working ideal; and a hipper version is again very possible through awareness, dedication, and hard work. Chores that benefit success are not chores at all, but labors of love and promise.

Speaking of Mayberry RFD, in a small town in Michigan, around September of 2009, there was a news story (AP) concerning a woman in a middle-class neighborhood who would let the neighborhood children gather at her house for fifteen minutes or so to wait for the school bus. She was a good neighbor just helping out the other mothers in the area as they had to go to work. Apparently she got a reprimand from the State, saying she did not have a license for a daycare facility, and she could not shelter these children for the fifteen to thirty minutes it took for the school bus to arrive each day. If she continued to do this, she could face up to ninety days in jail and/ or a thousand-dollar fine. She did not want or accept any monetary compensation for this act, as she was just being a good neighbor. Is this the kind of control we want from our governments?

This is an example of a state government that has way overstepped its bounds. This is what happens when the good acts of our neighbors are squelched by local government bureaucracy and control. What happens when it infiltrates the federal system? Is that not an indicator toward a Socialist form of government? How dear are your freedoms? These are the questions we should ask ourselves.

Let us not look at the world from the perspectives of others but from the perspectives of Americans. Do we really want to be like other countries? Do we really want to give up all the things we have been granted under the Constitution? Do you really know what you have been endowed with under the Declaration of Independence?

Members of the United Kingdom do. Daniel Hannon, a Fox News contributor, wonders to this day what we are doing. Before you speak of regulation and the likeness America should share with other countries of the world, read the aforementioned documents, and then decide if you wish to give up all that is offered to you. The power and freedom that we hold can, and will under the correct vision, begin to nurture a world that can function with interconnectivity, allowing each member to control their own destiny through oversight and responsibility in the world community. Freedom can still set the example for the rest of the world, if we actually begin to share all its benefits and promote it with pride and justice. Let us show the world we can rise above adversity through free choice, rather than a government-planned agenda. Oversight, not regulation, will lead to the success of this country.

CHAPTER SEVEN

THE BLAME GAME:
WHAT IT MEANS TO US

How many of us have had a situation in our homes where our children have misbehaved, and when we confront them, they point a finger and say, "They started it!" or "It wasn't my fault!"?

Doesn't that seem eerily similar to Nancy Pelosi stating that while employed as Speaker of the House, she claimed that the CIA had not briefed her on the waterboarding issue? "It wasn't my fault. I was never briefed!" she said. Clearly the CIA has a protocol in place that requires them to brief Congress of any and all interrogation procedures, as these have to be approved by the legislative branch. This is a part of the checks and balances we mentioned in earlier chapters. Conveniently the Speaker, when confronted on this issue, had a temporary lapse of memory and placed the blame on the CIA. Convenient amnesia is no excuse. This is an injustice for American politics and simply a cheap diversionary tactic for the ineptitudes of the Speaker.

We as a society have embraced this sort of childlike behavior in our everyday life. It is easier to place blame on someone else than to deal with the imminent consequences due to our actions. Case in point: my boss had constructed some waterside structures without the necessary permits and was subsequently required to remove them. My boss had a conversation with a contractor to implement the work. No contract had been signed, so when he had showed up for the job, he asked just what needed to be done; and because I was on the site, I explained the details of the job based on what my boss told me. I was not aware of the conversation between my boss and the contractor and what, if anything, was agreed upon. The contractor performed all the work and presented a bill for his services.

My boss was upset at the cost and proceeded to accuse me of costing her too much money. The key here is that my boss did not communicate to me any limitations of cost, nor did she communicate this to the contractor. But she remains blameless in this issue because she has a scapegoat to hang the blame on. If she had only communicated some limits to either me or the contractor, there would have been no misunderstanding.

We have to remember that even if we are wrong, we can accept the responsibility of our actions. It is far better to recognize and accept our foibles and learn from them, than to force-feed our subordinates a dictatorial mind-set absent of acknowledgement.

In the first three months of the Obama administration, he had blamed the Bush presidency how many times? Honestly, I have lost count; but at some point you have to be able to realize that you have control now, and the results of the past are in your hands, and you will accept it carte blanche. No further blame is necessary except in the form of your own reflection of the handling of the instance at hand, unless you wish to play the "blame game" as some of our legislators have a propensity to do.

The blame game is a cover for a lack of insight of what to do in a particular situation. We all have done it, mostly in our youth and many times in adulthood. It manifests itself in the souls of individuals who feel out of their element and not in complete control of the situation. When confronted, we have a tendency to put forth blame and somehow bide some time to weave a fabricated, inherited, or imaginary situation that we feel comfortable to explain or rectify. President GW Bush blamed the entrance into the Iraq war on "bad intelligence" from the CIA. (Apparently Speaker Pelosi has taken a page from the same playbook.) The poor CIA has seemingly taken its place as the whipping boy for the executive and legislative branches of late, but I am sure they will survive.

The problem with the blame game is, it is easy to get caught up in this again and again. It would be interesting if like Pinocchio, people would grow a larger nose every time they passed on their responsibility and played the blame game. I could get a kick out of watching Speaker Pelosi's nose grow an inch or two on camera every time she tries to weasel out of a situation. Nancy Pelosi spent much time trying to blame the difficulty in passing the health care initiative on the insurance companies. Now I may not like the premiums that my insurance company charges for health care, but the company is only responding to the monetary risks they have to encounter by frivolous lawsuits brought before them by the same deadbeats who had sued McDonald's for unlabeled hot coffee cups and won. Why doesn't Congress address the issue of lawsuits? I believe because they are lawmakers and do not want to ostracize any legal constituency that may contribute to the reelection coffers.

After the president and Congress finish spending the stimulus money and inflation begins to climb through the roof, who are they going to blame this on? Even with a decrease in unemployment rates, when a government prints more money than it has assets, the price of the dollar overseas plummets; and we have gross inflation. I suppose we could blame the International Monetary Fund, or perhaps this is part of the plan from Secretary Geithner.

Conspiracy theory one: He had been in communication with other world leaders considering a global monetary system other than the dollar, so why would he want a strong dollar if we are to replace it with a lesser valued world currency? He could explain to the American people that the world economy became too strong against the dollar, and a new global currency would even the economic playing field, placing blame on devalued American goods. Unfortunately this would begin to dismantle our industrial productivity such as it is. Although currently, 90 percent of US jobs are in the service sector, so I would think that industrially we are headed south down the road toward Nicaragua.

As we begin to explore these so-called conspiracy theories or, as I like to call them, possibilities, we can see how our constitutional rights can slowly be taken away by this current administration right before our eyes. Why does this administration insist on pushing through huge legislation without the opportunity for it to be read or debated? Rep. John Conyers (Michigan) stated on television that the Democratic health care bill was too big to read, and he did not have the time or the lawyers, but he was going to vote for it anyway. He actually had the audacity to blame the authors of the bill for his laziness. He did not even push off the vote until he was able to read it, he just voted for it carte blanche. This type of action by the people who are elected to represent us is simply unconscionable.

The DNC has put forth a smear campaign toward the people who have attended the town meetings during the congressional recess, calling them angry mobs and having manufactured anger. They accuse the GOP of bussing in the "mobs" to disrupt the meetings. This administration has even created a behavioral research czar to analyze the effects the town meetings are having on the administration's plans. If you research any protests online organized by the unions or ACORN or other left-wing factions, you will see folks wearing T-shirts carrying manufactured signs and chanting predetermined orations during their protests. The so-called right-wing "manufactured" town hall meetings had none of that. People showed up in their work clothes, carrying home-made signs, and spoke in quivering voices from the heart. If I were to compare the two types of events, my conclusion would be that the town meetings were uncontrived and a real snapshot of the controversy unfolding before the current administration of late.

Janeane Garofalo, Democrat, Hollywood icon, stated this on national TV concerning the health care town hall meetings, and I quote, "This is about hating a black man in the White House. This is racism straight up. This is nothing but a bunch of tea-bagging rednecks" (video from Fox News, August 5, 2009).

Ms. Garofalo and the DNC need to realize whitey gets it. Racial issues in this country at this time are more likely to be manufactured by members of ethnic factions than the general white population. We did learn from Dr. King the lessons of racial equality. Yet even Professor Gates and President Obama chose to place the race issue before the mainstream media in a scenario that was questionable at best. I would have expected better from two men with such esteemed educational pedigrees. One may agree with Ms. Garofalo, but with what insight?

I for one take huge offense at this "pinheaded" interpretation of American freedoms in action. This is Hollywood's version of character assassination. We voted for this man by 70 percent, not on his ethnic background but because of his political promises. Some may loathe him, but only by the lack of execution of his promises, not the color of his skin. If this country slithers toward racism, it is not because of the Anglo-Saxon community in this country; it is because of the special interests trying to divide this great union. The mainstream media and Hollywood have embraced this polarizing agenda, as the right-wing commentators try to understand it. How could a man voted into office by 70 percent of the vote be a victim of widespread racism? Give the president credit; he has remained above the fray—almost (Gates-gate.)

Yet the mainstream media and Hollywood are strong to perpetuate the story. Bill Maher also assaulted the American people as he called us "stupid and moronic." President Obama stated the Cambridge police department acted "stupidly" in the Professor Gates saga. Is there a theme here? My message to the Hollywood and Washington elitists is this: sticks and stones may break our bones, but names will never hurt us. I will let them know however that I agree with the Teddy Roosevelt premise of walking softly and carrying a big stick, even if he was a progressive. Please knock before entering my home.

Congratulations to those of you who question the actions of our elected officials. Thank heavens you remember that they work *for you*. Stand tall and raise your tea bags high, for there are some who want you to succumb to an alternative America devoid of the freedoms that you and I hold so dear.

What happens when our elected officials continually place their own faults on the shoulders of others? They try to convince us that they have our best interests at heart, and some other entity is engaged in some subversive scheme to undermine their plan. They begin to devise elaborate stories of the difficulty that has come about toward achieving our goals and that an alternative plan could be far better for us, although it may be far too complex for us to understand. When we question such a scheme, they publicly humiliate us by calling us "stupid and moronic" or an "angry mob."

The legislature is disingenuous toward the public reaction of health care and arrogantly blames the public for their reaction toward this behavior. Talk about being out of touch with your constituency. The White House Press Secretary Robert Gibbs even blames cable television for the high-octane reactions toward the legislature in these town hall meetings. This is clearly an administration either out of touch or wrongfully defiant toward the public.

In a rather unrelated story from May 2007, another example of the blame game that is out of control in our society has to do with a Little League case settled out of court. In Staten Island, New York, a child playing Little League got injured sliding into second base. It appears that the family of this child sued Little League Baseball Inc. and the New Springville Little League for $125,000, claiming that negligent coaching and the use of stationary bases were the cause of her son's injuries. The defendants stated that the child was indeed taught the proper technique for sliding, and the "soft touch" pop-up bases were also compliant with all safety standards.

The tragedy here is the fact that Little League Baseball Inc. settled out of court because of the chance of a massive lawsuit if they lost at trial. The attorney stated it was better to settle than go to trial and get socked for millions. Other attorneys have made similar statements like, "I tell my family: don't go before a jury." Wait a minute, isn't that why we have a judicial system and trial by jury, so we have a chance to defend ourselves against those who unjustly accuse us? This fear of justice by jury is caused by trial lawyers seeking grossly inflated awards in the courtroom. Don't you think Congress could pass some legislation to put caps on some of these cases? Oh, silly me, most of them *are* lawyers, aren't they? Go figure. *Vote for tort reform!*

I am tired of this blame game. I hope we all can come to terms with our ineptitudes, learn from them, and accept them. After all, we are inherently human; and with that will come success and inevitably some failure. I dislike the fact that some countries blame the United States for whatever propaganda they wish to peddle to their masses. Recently the Venezuelan government has called our past president "the devil" and has blamed the United States for its failed programs.

I am against anyone foreign or domestic who wishes to deface our commander in chief. I took issue with the leftists who published a picture of President George W. Bush as the Joker from the Batman movies. Of course the rightists did the same to Obama, which was quite unimaginative and equally disturbing. Now we have seen depictions of the current president dressed in a Nazi uniform, sporting a Hitleresque moustache and surrounded by swastikas. I stand tall and proud with the Democrats in condemning this depiction of our commander in chief. After all, Hitler was a Fascist, not a Communist.

If we begin to look at American history from the 1930s, we can begin to see how the progressive movements have polarized the two parties against each other. By the fifties, there were signs of both the Communist influence and the Nazi influence in the Democratic and Republican parties respectively. Rallies were held with swastikas, and hammer and sickles displayed next to statues of George Washington and other founding fathers right here on American soil. We know that the Communists and the Nazis hated each other because they both wanted totalitarian control over their citizens and the world. The Nazis wanted to take control with a Fascist modus operandi, while the Communists used a technique from within the government to slowly begin dismantling the codes of responsibility by pursuing their agenda under the guise of equality for all, or redistribution of wealth.

Certainly this could be taken out of context from our own Constitution, or even our Pledge of Allegiance to our flag—*"liberty and justice for all . . ."* The fact of the matter is that the progressive members of both parties for many decades have embraced ideals from some of the most polarizing and totalitarian entities in the world—the Nazi Party for the Republicans and the Communist Party for the Democrats.

Let's take the decision of the last Bush administration (Bush 43) to retaliate after September 11, 2001. We started with Afghanistan to get Osama bin Laden, so how did we end up in Iraq? What was the premise? WMDs, or divide and conquer? Isn't that what Hitler tried in Europe? Isn't this kind of a Fascist ideal, to go in militarily with a shock-and-awe mentality and no apparent reason? Why were we there?

Oh, don't smirk, my little blue dog Smurfs, your turn is coming.

Hitler and the Fascist regime failed due to their arrogant forthright march toward control. Their ego was way too big. They even had the Russians back on their heels until their scorched earth policy pretty much froze the Nazis out of Russia in WWII. Then in the postwar era, Communism reared its ugly head by marketing to the masses that they could have a better country if they all came together and shared the wealth the government had to offer. This is a fair and balanced lifestyle. Everyone makes the same, lives the same way, and those who currently make more, pay for those who don't. This was "hope and change" post-WWII.

Why does the Obama administration feel that the taxpayers need to bailout the banks, auto industry, and health care? Why is this administration going to raise taxes on the wealthy? Isn't this just the simple act of redistribution of wealth a simply Communist ideal?

I can see the blue fur ruffling and hear the *harrumphs* from the other side. You want to make me stop?

BRING BACK MY CONSTITUTION!
(Yes, the one written 233 years ago in Philadelphia)

I'm not blaming the GOP or the Democrats for their actions. The slow loss of our freedoms is our cross to bear and ours alone. These progressives truly believe in a different America than our founding fathers, and if we let them change it, they will. If I leave my Ferrari (provided I owned one) parked on the side of the street in a neighborhood known for its unsavory characters and leave it unlocked with the keys in it, I have no one to blame but myself when I return and find it missing. You wouldn't leave the doors to your house unlocked or the alarm unarmed in a bad neighborhood. So why let unsavory politicians tinker with your freedoms and not hold them accountable?

We must remember to ask ourselves these questions and remember that the Constitution and the Bill of Rights are gifts for the *people,* not the government. If we let go of it, others will take it away from us and replace it with something of their own making. Those who would so easily steal our freedoms will be much less likely to return them to us.

CHAPTER EIGHT

THEY HAVE AWAKENED THE SLEEPING GIANT

Yes, it is true. Part of this electorate has indeed begun to stir. The health care debate has awakened large numbers of Americans who finally figured out that the Grinch has stolen their comfy little pillow, and the coffee is all gone. If this were my house, that would make for one very "cranky Yankee." The "tea parties" were a good idea to enlighten the electorate to the gross mismanagement of this administration, and the Democrats helped by trying to push through a 2,400-page health care reform bill right in front of our noses. Thank you, Rep. Conyers, for stating that the bill was too big to read, but you'll vote for it anyway. (My tongue is planted firmly in my cheek.)

This bill is so economically massive that even banks are skeptical to lend to small businesses until it is settled. When a government program is so big it scares the financial sector, we definitely need to wake up. President Obama has stated that no one wants to kill Grandma, but his program appears not to kill her, just ration her care until God takes her before her time. That must be the eloquent difference between acts of God and government meddling in the health care system.

Well, at last there is an issue that seems to excite the American people. Now before we all go off half-cocked, let's start thinking about steps toward a reasonable solution for this and all the other things that have happened in these past few months. You know, something that won't break the budget and leave us in Third World heaven controlled by thirty-two different czars who answer to no one. (Can you believe it? Just over two years. It seems like an eternity.)

The many polls that track everything from how much we weigh to what is the most popular color in America have a general consensus that the president's job approval rating is falling faster than mercury in Siberia during winter. How can that be? We voted for him overwhelmingly in the general election. It appears, my friends, that beautiful words filled with "hope and change" cannot compete with the cold hard facts such as increasing unemployment, manufactured money, an absent foreign policy, failed auto industry, failed banking industry, and a commitment into a war we are not expected to win, just to name a few. Oh hell, did I mention the largest national debt in our history, and he added a massive health care bill on top of that? That would put this country in such a debt that it would take decades of huge sacrifice just to break even.

As an average American, I feel that the president does not speak to the public as a communicator, but that he *campaigns* to the public from his office. FDR had his fireside chats, and JFK, Nixon, and Reagan spoke to the American public directly. This president only seems to know how to campaign. His diatribes are not from the heart, but from some prepared speech meant to incite and please regardless of full disclosure. This is not unlike Caesar, Stalin, Hitler, Napoleon, and other prominent leaders from history.

History will tell you that most Socialist countries became Socialist not by choice, but by necessity. They either failed through a corrupt monarchy, or were wartorn and had nothing left, or some other catastrophic incident. Socialism is nothing more than a cancerous legion on a free society. Are Nancy Pelosi, Harry Reid, and the Obama administration actually trying to disrupt the country so badly that they can rebuild it in their own vision? Don't scoff, this is a viable question. After the "shellacking" the president got in 2010, he now has begun to compromise a little. We need to keep our guard up so to speak because the same major players who angered us in 2009 are still there. This compromise is a ploy to get a second term, to assuage the republic, and then deploy his agenda in 2012 when there is nothing for him to lose. He gets to retire on four hundred thousand dollars a year for life while we get to live with his policies and the taxpayer burden of redistribution of wealth.

I had been in the health care field as a CT tech for about ten years before I got so fed up with it. I made mistakes and changed direction. That could be another story for another time. One thing I remember is the intrusion that a cancerous legion can wield. If it moves quickly, it can literally put the caregivers back on their heels. If it moves slowly, it can eat away one's body quietly and without warning. Either way, the result is the same—death.

The key to avoiding death is twofold. First, we need to understand the nature of the cancer and then aggressively and systematically take steps to stop its progression until it is gone. Within our republic, the "tea party" movement has taken that first step. They have lessened the progressives' control of the House of Representatives. This may not be a total cure, but it will, at the very least, bide time to seek alternative actions if one chooses to continue.

This administration has unknowingly defined itself as a "cancer" on the Constitution of the United States of America and the public ideal as we know it. The current administration has created an enormous debt; and feeding on change and community organization, it has grown in size to a massive bureaucracy and wormed its way into the banking industry and auto industry, and is trying to metastasize to the health care industry. This is a very aggressive tumor set to attack the lifeblood of our liberty.

In cancer therapy, we have an arsenal of weapons to combat the tumor, and so it should be the same for this or any other metastasis or permeation of our liberties. First, we need to identify the tumor and identify the vessels which feed it. Some tumors have been described as "leggy," meaning they have many tendrils tapping a blood supply and become very difficult to excise. Do you think an administration with thirty-two czars who have no one to answer to could be considered "leggy"? I know you see where I'm going with this.

Don't get me wrong, the previous administration was almost as bad, with the war on terror and all of its "special advisors." But these tendrils that we speak of today are manipulating their way into our Constitution disguised as unions and community organizations such as the ACLU, NAACP, ACORN, SEIU, APOLLO, and many others. They are taking your donations toward "hope and change" and feeding the new government with power and strength, creating strong lobbies under the direction of the current commander in chief and the House and Senate leaders. Perhaps in correlation to the sanctity of the Constitution, these three could be construed as the real "Axis of Evil," letting these czars operate as a shadow government and approving legislation without any oversight.

At last the public has begun to awaken and realize the programs being pushed through the Congress in the wee hours of the morning are suspicious at best. We now begin to understand the ideal of transparency, which was preached to us during the campaign, was nothing more than a smoke screen. Transparency in this administration is a very different thing than what you and I perceive; it is clouded with many panes of frosted glass. After all, how can one be transparent about bills that were never read? How can the president state on national TV that he is unaware of the illegal operations taking place within ACORN, an organization that was instrumental in getting him elected and is receiving billions in taxpayer money, which was the focus of a story that had been in the news for three weeks prior to his interview.

It is not enough to just be awakened, America. We now have to go to work. We have to study and identify the bills that threaten our liberties and speak long and loud against such blasphemy. We also have to make viable suggestions to the members of Congress who will support our desires even if they are not our own representatives. Remember *freedom takes work*.

How do we do it? Use the same plan they used to blindside us. We start with a combination of the same rules that they used on us, Saul Alinsky's *Rules for Radicals* (Random House, 1971). Let's start with rule number eleven, "Pick the target, freeze it, personalize it, and polarize it. Identify a responsible individual. Ignore attempts to shift or spread the blame." Follow by rule number eight, "Keep the pressure on . . ." Once we have identified the culprits, we can begin to isolate and freeze them, and begin to dismantle their work systematically and, more important, legally.

So who are these people who strive to control our freedoms? Some would believe that it is President Obama, but what of Nancy Pelosi or Harry Reid? Lesson number one, if it appears too obvious, it probably is; so rest easy all of you who voted for Obama. You merely put in place a community organizer who is nothing more than a puppet in the White House, and a couple of feral and liberal Democrats in Congress who are nothing more than children in a candy shop with their own credit card (which you cosigned for by the way.) This is still a very dangerous situation for the Constitution.

Lesson number two, if you want to find corruption, you must follow the money or the power; both will lead to the same place.

Liberal Democrats in both houses and the White House have relinquished their responsibilities in writing legislation and handed it off to someone else. The stimulus package wasn't written by any member of Congress, it was written by members of the Apollo Alliance, a "coalition of labor, business, environmental, and community leaders working to catalyze a clean energy revolution" who represent special interests and have close ties to ACORN. Did you know the stimulus gave billions of dollars to ACORN? Why?

Another question that should be asked is why a clean energy coalition is writing stimulus legislation for Congress. I thought that is what the Congress was supposed to do. Sounds fishy? According to the Apollo Alliance website, they developed the "New Apollo Program," which is a plan to *identify priorities for federal action and investment, including a "cap and invest" program to reduce carbon emissions.* Gee, and you thought your government was working for you.

Let's talk about our commander in chief for a moment; this email was sent to me as a narrative from a *Washington Post* story authored by Dale Lindsborg.

The following is a narrative taken from a 2008 Sunday morning televised *Meet the Press*. The author (Dale Lindsborg) is employed by none other than the very liberal *Washington Post*!

From Sunday's 07 Sept. 2008 11:48:04 EST, Televised *Meet the Press*. THE THEN Senator Obama was asked about his stance on the American Flag.

General Bill Ginn USAF (ret.) asked Obama to explain WHY he doesn't follow protocol when the National Anthem is played. The General stated to Obama that according to the United States Code, Title 36, Chapter 10, Sec. 171 ... During rendition of the national anthem, when the flag is displayed, all present (except those in uniform) are expected to stand at attention facing the flag with the right hand over the heart. Or, at the very least, "Stand and Face It." Now get this ...

'Senator' Obama replied:

"As I've said about the flag pin, I don't want to be perceived as taking sides." There are a lot of people in the world to whom the American flag is a symbol of oppression. The anthem itself conveys a war-like message. You know, the bombs bursting in air and all that sort of thing.

(ARE YOU READY FOR THIS?)

Obama continued: "The National Anthem should be 'swapped' for something less parochial and less bellicose. I like the song 'I'd Like To Teach the World To Sing.' If that were our anthem, then, I might salute it. In my opinion, we should consider reinventing our National Anthem as well as 'redesign' our Flag to better offer our enemies hope and love. It's my intention, if elected, to disarm America to the level of acceptance to our Middle East Brethren. If we, as a Nation of warring people, conduct ourselves like the nations of Islam, where peace prevails—perhaps a state or period of mutual accord could exist between our governments."

"When I become President, I will seek a pact of agreement to end hostilities between those who have been at war or in a state of enmity, and a freedom from disquieting oppressive thoughts. We as a Nation, have placed upon the nations of Islam, an unfair injustice which is WHY my wife disrespects the Flag and she and I have attended several flag burning ceremonies in the past."

"Of course now, I have found myself about to become the President of the United States and I have put my hatred aside. I will use my power to bring CHANGE to this Nation, and offer the people a new path. My wife and I look forward to becoming our Country's First black Family. Indeed, CHANGE is about to overwhelm the United States of America."

Flag burnings—really.

I have problems with anyone disrespecting the flag, and I have problems with *change* about to *overwhelm* the United States of America.

Wake up, America. It gets worse. Van Jones, the green jobs czar, in an interview with the *East Bay Express* in 2005 made some frightening admissions about his rise to power. He was arrested twice, once in 1993 after the riots in San Francisco, when the police were acquitted in the Rodney King case. The second time was in 1999 during the protests in Seattle against the World Trade Organization. Concerning the 1993 arrest, Van Jones stated, "In jail I met all these young radicals of color. I mean, really radical Communists and anarchists. I was like . . . this is what I need to be a part of." He also continued, "I spent the next ten years of my life working with a lot of these people I met in jail, trying to be a revolutionary." In the months that followed those protests, he explained further, "I was a rowdy nationalist on April 28. Then the verdict came down on April 29. By August *I was a Communist.*"

So now we have had an avowed Communist working in the higher echelons of government. Although he has since resigned, this was a person the administration liked to advise the president. Could it get any worse? He did not have to go through any FBI clearance to get the job. It appears that either President Obama or Rahm Emanuel had been pushing to have these czars in place without FBI inspection. By the way, Rahm Emanuel has since resigned as well, although not at the president's request. To make matters even more bizarre, Eric Holder, the attorney general of the United States, has begun a probe of the CIA over the terrorist interrogation techniques of the Bush administration.

Pardon me a moment while I climb on my soapbox. What is going on here? First, the general public has no need to know anything about military interrogation techniques that take place, especially those that take place *outside of United States soil!* Second, many more horrible tortures have been done to our soldiers overseas than waterboarding. As long as our techniques do not overstep the bounds set by the Geneva Convention, we as a populace need to keep our noses where they belong.

The CIA was founded to gather intelligence, so let them do their job. Giving someone a facial bath or threatening to kill their family is not deadly; uncomfortable maybe, but not deadly. When will the ACLU and others get it through their heads that these people are terrorists, and they would treat you worse if ever you had the gonads to serve your country and risk capture for the rights you utilize so freely? Perhaps you should realize that *war is hell.*

There, that felt good. Now, I do believe that interrogations should be done by the professionals who are supposed to do the job, not the soldiers and MPs at a temporary holding center like Abu Ghraib. Those ex-soldiers (yes, *ex*-soldiers—they do not deserve the recognition) fully deserved the punishments that were issued under the UCMJ. While I'm on the subject of terrorists, let's make one thing perfectly clear. Prisoners at the Guantanamo Bay detention facility in Cuba are *not* US citizens. Therefore they are *not* protected by the rights granted to the US citizenry under the US Constitution, nor should they be. These folks are foreign prisoners who tried to do harm to the people of the United States. They should remain off our sovereign soil and tried by a war crime tribunal under the rules of the Geneva Convention. They should *never* be allowed on this soil and *never* be given rights under the US Constitution.

The idea to close the Guantanamo Bay detention facility and send these terrorists to our public prisons is ludicrous at best. Remember Van Jones, the self-proclaimed Communist? He learned a lot from the people in prison. You think the terrorists wouldn't try to teach their cell mates who might be eligible for parole that jihad against America would be more successful from inside the country? These folks are masters at brainwashing young angry impressionable minds, and I think it could be safe to say most prisoners are at least a little bit angry. Do we really want to have our prisoners communing with the likes of those who sent three aircraft into key targets on September 11, 2001, and killed thousands of innocent people just going about their business?

Apparently the current administration feels that we should. Some members of Congress have even sung the praises of Fidel Castro and Hugo Chavez of Venezuela. Remember Chavez kept calling President Bush "El Diablo" as he killed thousands of his own countrymen and tried to do away with the term limits for the presidency? Well, there are members of the Congress and special advisors to the president who outwardly support these leaders.

Diane Watson (Democrat, California) for one, and I quote from her recent speech, "And I want you to know, now, you can think whatever you want about Fidel Castro, but he was one of the brightest leaders I have ever met. And you know, the Cuban revolution that kicked out the wealthy, Che Guevara did that, and then after they took over they went out among the population to find someone who could lead this new nation, and they found well, an attorney by the name of Fidel Castro."

Call me silly, but they had a revolution, kicked out all the wealthy, and then just found this attorney to run the country? I live in Florida now, and the boats just keep coming from ninety miles away. If life is so grand in Cuba, why are there so many people trying to leave? Answer that, Diane Watson.

Mark Lloyd, the FCC diversity czar, likes some of the aspects of Hugo Chavez and the last Venezuelan revolution, especially the part where the government silenced and shut down all access to the media. According to the website politics.gather.com, Mark Lloyd is quoted as saying, "It should be clear by now that my focus is not freedom of speech or the press." He continued, "This freedom is all too often an exaggeration. At the very least, blind references to freedom of speech or the press serve as a distraction from the critical examination of other communication policies."

OK, what other communication policies would we want besides freedom of speech and the press? Mark Lloyd has embraced a bill circulating in Congress to give the president control to monitor and shut down the Internet during a "cyberemergency." Senators Olympia Snowe (Democrat, Maine) and John Rockefeller (Democrat,

West Virginia) have negotiated tirelessly behind the scenes in Washington and have proposed a bill that allows the White House to seize temporary control of *private sector networks* during a so-called cyberemergency.

The new version of this bill will grant the president the right to declare a cybersecurity emergency relating to "non-governmental" computer networks and do what is necessary to respond to the *perceived* (not actual) threat. Other sections of the proposal include a federal certification program to train cybersecurity professionals to run certain systems and networks in the private sector if deemed necessary. The scary verbiage in this proposal goes something like this: The White House is supposed to engage in "periodic mapping" of the private networks deemed to be critical, and those companies "shall share" requested information with the federal government; talk about Big Brother. Here we see the broad brushstrokes of ambiguity within the bill, granting virtually unlimited powers to the government and those untethered czars who roam the halls of the White House having the ear of the president. The mainstream media was up in arms when the Bush administration tried to eavesdrop on the general public during the last administration. Why not now?

We also have Cass Sunstein, the information regulatory czar who is in favor of regulating speech on the Internet. He also believes animals should have the right to sue humans in court (say whaaaaat?). In his book *Democracy and the Problem of Free Speech* (Free Press, 1995), he believes that the Internet may weaken democracy because it allows citizens to isolate themselves within groups that share their own views and experiences, and thus cut themselves off from information that might challenge their beliefs. He claims this is a phenomenon known as *cyber-balkanization*. I would guess he doesn't have a Facebook page.

When my dad stopped at the diner every morning to discuss the current events with his friends, would Cass have found him to be *"diner-balkanized"*? Why on earth does this administration need multiple czars overseeing how information is relayed across a country that has a constitutional right of free speech and a free press? Sherlock Holmes might just have been inclined to say that something curious is afoot, my dear Watson.

It is time to take stock of just who and what has been implemented in these past few short months. We have had the government take over the banking industry and car industry, and increases to the debt that have brought us to unsustainable levels, allowing for a possible collapse of the dollar on the world market. There have been self-avowed Communists and Socialists placed in positions of great power without the blessings of the FBI, and huge policies voted upon in the wee hours of the night by a Congress who doesn't even have a chance to read the bills.

There was a promise from this president of "fundamentally transforming America," but what changes are we really talking about? The viewpoints of many of these czars were formed by the radical Left and in some cases by Communists, Socialists, and even anarchists. I don't know about you, but that kind of change is not what the founders wanted for America.

So what do we do?

First, educate yourself. All the information in this book came from public sites on the Internet and news agencies in a matter of minutes for each subject. You should hurry though, before the information regulatory czar tells the president there is a cyberemergency, and he shuts down the Internet.

Second, contact your legislators and request they stonewall any legislation put before them until they read and understand it. Make sure that private corporations do not write bills, but that your representatives in Washington do. Make certain that your senators and representatives uphold the Constitution of the United States by looking at their voting record on line. *You have a fundamental chance to change Congress this next election. Don't let it pass by.*

Remember free speech is a constitutional right, and there is a czar who believes his focus is *not* freedom of speech or the press. If we prevent our legislators from passing obtuse bills written by radicals from the left who want to slowly dismantle the constitution in order to have complete control of this country, we can systematically remove them from power through the electoral system of the people. That is the beauty of this magnificent document penned 233 years ago. We can request that our representatives uphold the Constitution, and if they do not, we vote them out. Their voting records are public knowledge, but it is up to us to research them before it is too late. The radicals in this administration are hoping that you remain complacent.

After the "shellacking" the president took in 2010, he has had a mellower tone, similar to Bill Clinton after his first term. Don't be fooled. President Obama is no Bill Clinton. Bill Clinton wanted a second term, but he was a southern Democrat who believed in the Constitution of the United States. He had to soften his agenda to pass legislation for his constituency. Barack Obama is presenting himself in the same manner for a very different outcome. Remember he has surrounded himself with left-wing *progressives* who, by studying Marx, Lenin, and Saul Alinsky, believe the Constitution is an ineffective document. They believe that capitalism is a crime.

If President Obama gets reelected, he has *carte blanche* power to continue to "fundamentally transform America." Honestly, he has nothing to lose, only a legacy to gain. He even gets a full paycheck for the rest of his life, paid by us the taxpayer. Do you *really* want to reward someone for turning us into China, France, or Greece? I don't know about you; but I like being free, prosperous, and respectful of others in the world. I don't want to snub my nose at the rest of the world, but I don't feel I have to be just like them either.

America should lead by example. We should be respectful and tolerant, but ready and strong. There is nothing wrong with being a superpower, as long as "you walk softly and carry a big stick." Let us not dismantle the greatest nation in the world for some Socialist utopian ideal that has never been proven viable.

It is not enough to just contact your legislators. We must begin to think like a legislator, and a good one. Think of the issues that affect you, and what could be done to solve the problems which bother you. Take an issue and apply it to your own lifestyle. Bring everything into a perspective such as, don't think of the economy in trillions, but in hundreds. Think of how you would provide solutions to balance your own checkbook. Think about how you would like to see your child educated. Have you noticed that our legislators never discuss the concept of the three R's anymore (Reading, wRiting, and aRithmetic)? Why don't we concentrate a little more on simple fundamentals for the sake of our children? We do not have to provide all the answers, but if we let our legislators know our feelings and concerns, it enables them to devise a plan that may be a closer resemblance to a viable solution.

One thing I am in support of is term limits for both the House and Senate. The Constitution grants them unlimited terms, and a change would have to be ratified by a two-thirds majority as an amendment. That could be a big hill to climb, but not impossible. Persistent and rational arguments to your legislators could just persuade them to vote for it.

What about welfare? As a working self-employed capitalist, why do I have to pay for folks who sit in front of the TV day after day and collect a paycheck for doing nothing? Why don't we try this: If you fall from grace and lose your job, (and we all have) we as a citizenry will allow our government to support you for a maximum of two years.

Two years are enough to garner an associate's degree, to retrain yourself in a more marketable skill set. You can get a certificate program for much less time and money. The government will allow a 0 percent interest rate on that student loan for a designated term. If you fail to repay the debt, the government may garnish wages. You can spend the money anyway you wish however, but your benefit is based on your family need at the time of application. This means that if you spit out more children in that two-year span, the money does not increase. Condoms and abstinence would be my personal choice if you are financially strapped. After you have utilized the government program, you may not reapply for compensation for a period of seven years. If you are injured and cannot work in that time, utilize catastrophic insurance.

This welfare-to-work program may seem harsh to the progressive movement, but it is a practical measure to stimulate a feeling of self-worth to those who either have made mistakes or those who are victims of a society gone awry. This is a statement toward recovery, both personal and national in nature.

Health care has some huge issues that need to be addressed. This issue is far too big to take on in a single session, although we have to start somewhere. Let's try tort reform. If we can put a cap on wrongful death, we can leverage insurance companies to drop malpractice rates to affordable levels so doctors can practice medicine under the Hippocratic oath they believe in without the threat of bankruptcy. The lower litigation costs will trickle down to the insurance companies, who will lower costs in a competitive market and allow treatments to flow faster and more efficiently. This will translate into more money in the system for Medicare and Medicaid, and with an option to purchase drugs from Canada, this will create a competitive market for the pharmaceutical industry as well. Insurance companies also need to be able to market beyond state lines and help the consumer by increasing competition and driving down costs. This is capitalism at its very best.

Let's initiate a flat tax on all US citizens and require a balanced budget amendment to make this country live within its means. Temporary tax increases can be approved by special session for times of war or other extenuating circumstances voted on by the public.

We had some success in the election before last, persuading candidates to not take monies from lobbyists. If we can continue that pressure with our current legislators by requesting them to sign a pledge to refuse money from organized lobbies and unions, and/or vote for a reasonable cap on such organized campaign contributions, it would go a long way to cutting abuse. I would go further to request that all campaign contributions be given by a cashier's check to keep the donors anonymous. Then the support is based on the candidates' platform, not the underhanded deals and payback that come from corporate and lobbyist contributions.

If lobbyists are to plead their cases to our legislators, let them do it as an attorney would plead his case to a jury, without the weapon of millions of dollars in campaign contributions. How would we make this work and be regulated? I'm not quite sure. Perfect solutions begin with imperfect ideas, but it is a start. The voices of the common American are what this country was founded on, and we can again take control of our freedoms and our liberties against a coercive shadow government that seeks to undermine the US Constitution and relinquish every American's rights, for the achievement of a Socialist ideology.

When I was ten or twelve, my mother took me into the voting booth with her during one presidential election. Although I did not understand all the detail of the issues at hand, I remember to this day watching her, the two of us behind the curtain as she happily fulfilled her obligation to America. I recall receiving a small American flag as we exited the polling place. It is up to us to ensure that we bring our children to vote, and let them see democracy at work in real time. Answer their questions honestly, and teach them the importance of this crucial right.

Next, we are a Christian nation. We were founded on Christian values by brave souls who believed in God and fought for him to be in our lives. Although we are also a melting pot, we should never forget from whence we came. If I travel to India, I do not expect them to relinquish their Hindu beliefs for mine, yet we as a nation under the direction of the left have seemingly little regard for our Christian values and cater to those of other religious beliefs in the name of religious equality. We need to accept the religious beliefs of others who travel here but never ever relinquish our Christian values for them. I believe that "In God We Trust" should remain a sovereign motto for this country and should be respected by all who choose to live here.

Each of us has a duty to take responsibility for the continued construction of this country, by becoming engaged in what we vote for and following through to check on our governing body. I truly believe there are good souls in our government who have slid off the righteous road of service to the people, for the corruption of wealth or power or both. It is up to us to remain vigilant and hold these people accountable to uphold the greatest document of freedom ever written—the Constitution of the United States of America.

Last, I wish to reinstate the Pledge of Allegiance in our schools. Can someone please explain to me or you, why we don't recite it anymore? As a matter of fact, I believe every day of every session of Congress should include and begin with a verbal recitation of the Pledge of Allegiance to remind our legislators who they work for.

Say it with me:

"I pledge allegiance to the flag of the United States of America. And to the Republic for which it stands one nation under God, indivisible, for freedom and justice for all."

EPILOGUE

I can't forget, I am a sole architect, I built the shadows here, I built the growling voice I fear . . .

—Excerpt from the song "Hey Pretty,"
off the CD *Haunted* by Poe